Advance Praise for

EXIT-READY MARKETING

"In numerous cases, I've witnessed Shiv's framework deliver more predictable revenue, higher pipeline coverage, better conversion rates, lower customer acquisition costs, and higher net retention rates. These outcomes mean substantial value for a business at exit."

—**ZANE TARENCE**, Partner and
Managing Director of Founders Advisors

"Shiv does an amazing job in *Exit-Ready Marketing* of making very complex analysis and strategies seem simple. I highly recommend it for founders, CEOs, and investors looking to professionalize and accelerate their marketing efforts."

—**BRYCE YOUNGREN**, Managing Partner at Polaris Growth Fund

"An essential guide for founders to skyrocket their valuation."

—**NEIL PATEL**, Co-Founder of Neil Patel Digital

"The best companies run their Go-To-Market like a revenue factory. Shiv's framework offers founders and executives a data- and process-driven approach to revenue growth that not only enhances valuation but also ensures sustainable and durable growth."

—**JACCO VAN DER KOOIJ**, Founder of Winning by Design

"I want every founder to get every penny they can when they exit. You do that by reading and implementing what's inside this book. Shiv has laid everything out in a step-by-step process to help you understand how private equity investors buy and sell companies, and he tells you exactly what they're looking for in simple mathematical terms and easy-to-use frameworks."

—**DAN MARTELL**, Founder of SaaS Academy

"*Exit-Ready Marketing* gets you in the head of the PE playbook for GTM that investors use to get more value from your company *after* you sell. Read this book now and get that value for yourself."

—**KEVIN MOSLEY**, General Partner at Jurassic Capital

"Marketing ROI has been a black box for too many for too long. Shiv Narayanan demystifies how companies can leverage marketing to create enterprise value."

—**MATT GALLAGHER**, Portfolio CRO at Hg Capital

"As a growth equity investor, the concepts Shiv speaks to in this book—ICP, demand gen, pipeline conversion, sales enablement, and revenue operations—are exactly the stuff we spend time on with our portfolio companies. Predictability in your sales pipeline is everything—it gives you the ability to see ahead and allows you to thoughtfully plan and invest in your business. It can exponentially charge the growth trajectory of a business and therefore its valuation. This book should be required reading for all bootstrapped tech founders, especially those who haven't grown up in sales and marketing."

—**VAIBHAV NALWAYA**, Co-Founder and Managing Partner at Wavecrest Growth Partners

"Few CEOs, CFOs, and investors truly understand the marketing function or how to evaluate it. In this book, Shiv Narayanan provides a structured framework on the nine key elements that are critical to get right and then provides criteria on how to evaluate them as well as an end-to-end case study to bring it all to life."

—**AJ GANDHI**, Chief Growth Officer at Marlin Equity Partners

"Everything you need to professionalize your marketing and prepare for an eventual exit. A must-read for all founders."

—**ERIC SIU**, CEO of Single Grain

"Shiv's insights are the difference between a standard exit and a killer valuation. Don't exit without them."

—**WES BUSH**, Founder and CEO of ProductLed

EXIT-READY MARKETING

THE 9-STEP FRAMEWORK TO MAXIMIZE YOUR VALUATION

Shiv Narayanan

LIONCREST
PUBLISHING

EXIT-READY MARKETING
The 9-Step Framework to Maximize Your Valuation
First Edition

Author Photograph: Katy Chan

ISBN   978-1-5445-4608-7   *Hardcover*
       978-1-5445-4610-0   *Paperback*
       978-1-5445-4609-4   *Ebook*

CONTENTS

FOREWORD
by Dan Martell

Dan Martell is the author of the Wall Street Journal *bestseller* Buy Back Your Time. *After founding, scaling, and successfully exiting three technology companies, he was named Canada's top angel investor in 2012. A few years later, Dan founded SaaS Academy, now one of the world's largest coaching companies. He's also an Ironman athlete, philanthropist, husband, and father of two incredible boys.*

TRIPLE YOUR COMPANY'S VALUE

A few years ago, I bought a company in the automotive space. The founder was a brilliant, hard-working guy. He knew his industry inside and out. He knew his product inside and out. And he was ready to *cash out*.

I dug around the financial details, "kicked the tires" of the product and the business model, and made an offer. We negotiated, then agreed.

But you know what? He could have gotten *three times more money.*

I didn't rip him off, no one did anything shady, and while I'd like to think I'm a pretty good negotiator, my negotiation skills weren't the reason he sold for far less than he should have.

Why didn't he get more money? Because his business lacked something critical—predictable pipeline and revenue. He had huge differences in his revenue every month, and he was relying on a handful of customers for a bulk of the volume. In short, revenue quality was the reason I couldn't pay a higher valuation for his business. Any wise investor is going to back away quickly from that kind of risk or at least shortchange him for it in his exit valuation.

As an investor, it's frustrating to see companies with huge potential that aren't converting that potential into enterprise value. But as a founder, I completely understand. With the day-to-day grind and urgent tasks pulling him in different directions, taking that step back and working *on* his business rather than *in* the business can get pushed far down the list of priorities.

As soon as I bought the business, I made major changes that he could have easily made to increase the amount I paid to acquire the business. I spent three months improving the foundational elements of the company's Go-To-Market. And in short order, we multiplied revenue by 300 percent.

That's how it happens. Founders, every day, miss something foundational, and then, when it's time to sell, they miss out on half or more of the money they should have received, if they sell at all.

I don't want you to make his mistake. In fact, I don't want *him* to make his mistake again. I want every founder to get every penny they can when they exit.

You do that by reading and implementing what's inside this book. Shiv has laid everything out in a step-by-step process to help you understand how private equity (PE) investors buy and sell companies, and he tells you exactly what they're looking for in simple mathematical terms and easy-to-use frameworks.

What many founders don't realize is that marketing can be their key to driving predictable revenue. They see it as a cost center, or a distraction from sales efforts. As Shiv will show you, with the right strategy, any business can professionalize their marketing and turn it into a phenomenal growth lever. Shiv helps you to get the right data, understand what it's saying about your business, and act on these insights. The frameworks in *Exit-Ready Marketing* are actionable for businesses of all sizes and industries, and you can start executing many of them as soon as you put down the book.

If you put off working on the areas Shiv highlights in this book, you'll end up paying a high price—in terms of what investors are eventually willing to pay for your business. Going through the acquisition process is tough. Going through it only to have it fall through or to accept a disappointing valuation? It's brutal.

And even if you *don't* want to sell your company, a business others want to buy is one you want to run. Plain and simple.

Everything Shiv teaches in this book is brought straight down from the PE clouds, where he works with some of the largest investors in the world every day. He takes their complex thinking and simplifies it into easy-to-use frameworks every founder, entrepreneur, and operator can use.

If the entrepreneur who founded the automotive company I bought had read this book, he may never have sold it. Or, at least when he did, he would have tripled his valuation.

Exit-Ready Marketing shows you how investors see your business and takes the guesswork out of getting your business acquired. More than that, this book shows you in practical terms what you can do to secure the exit you and your business deserve.

INTRODUCTION

"The deal fell apart last Sunday," said David. "They gave me the news two weeks before we were supposed to close."

"What happened?" I asked.

"After looking through the data room, they said our revenue was too lumpy and our Go-To-Market was too unpredictable."

David was visibly frustrated. He had founded ClearTrack nine years ago and bootstrapped it to $7M in ARR, without any outside capital. On the personal front, he had two kids during the same time period and had just gone through a divorce. Meanwhile, a global pandemic happened, markets shifted, and the business went through several ups and downs.

It took blood, sweat, and tears to build the business to this point. He could have quit so many times along the way, but he never did. I felt his pain as an entrepreneur.

Founders like David put everything they've got into their businesses. They take salary cuts, accept personal financial risk, reinvest every dollar they earn, pay skyrocketing employee salaries to stay competitive, and try to manage cash flow to stay above water.

Their drivers for taking on all the stress? True belief in the mission of the business and deep care for the customers and employees they serve. Eventually, some founders are financially rewarded for creating so much value via an exit event, when they get to sell their business to a strategic or financial investor.

Such an event happens rarely, but when it does, it usually happens to a founder who was laser focused on serving others for an extended period, often for ten years or more. The financial windfall is a pleasant bonus that can transform the life of the founder and all the employees who helped build the business.

David was hoping to be one of those founders. At least he was until the deal fell apart.

Pinnacle Capital's feedback to David was that they liked the ClearTrack business and the market it was operating in, but they just couldn't get past the revenue numbers being all over the place every month.

"This is one of the most common reasons deals fall apart," I reassured David. "The fact that they got this deep in the process with you means they really wanted to buy this business. It also means we can turn this around."

I wasn't just trying to make David feel better about a missed opportunity of a lifetime. Pinnacle's reason for backing out is why so many private equity investors don't end up investing in companies after going through a due diligence phase.

The thing some founders don't realize is that investors like Pinnacle need to deploy their capital. Their entire business model revolves around raising capital from Limited Partners (LPs) to form a fund, finding good companies to invest in so they can deploy that capital, growing those companies to a point where they can eventually exit the investment for a significantly higher valuation, and ultimately returning the capital with those gains back to their LPs.

If they do a good job of going through this cycle enough times, they can generate a meaningful return for their LPs and then raise even more money to invest the next time around because LPs are more willing to trust them with larger amounts of capital.

This entire process depends on the private equity investor's ability to find and win deals. The market is super competitive because investors are often contending with each other for a limited supply of deals. The number of investors is increasing every year and so is the dry powder—the amount of uninvested capital raised by investors. As per Statista, the amount of uninvested capital in 2023 was nearly $3.9 trillion and continues to increase annually. Uninvested capital is the worst form of capital for an investor because that capital isn't working to generate a return.

So, when an investor decides not to invest or buy a company, it is not due to a lack of motivation.

In David's case, Pinnacle invested a lot of time and money into diligence to understand the business and then presented an internal pitch to their own investment committee on putting money into the business. Because ClearTrack's revenue was unpredictable, that investment committee passed.

ClearTrack's problem was that the revenue was just too lumpy. Some months, they were doing $15K in New MRR, while in others they were doing only $5K. It was hard to predict how much revenue each month would bring. David and his team had theories like seasonality or macro forces being the reasons why, but those factors didn't seem to fully explain the fluctuations, leaving them unable to pinpoint the reasons their revenue growth was sporadic.

This kind of unpredictability is an investor's worst nightmare. When they buy a business, their capital is tied up for years and they're committed till they can flip the investment. Revenue unpredictability signals a long slog of trying to figure out the business. It's just too risky. Investors would much rather wait for an investment with a healthier profile than take on that kind of risk.

"This is where your job as the founder is to build the right foundation for the business," I told David. "We need to make your revenue more predictable and show that there is a lot of upside left to be captured."

"How will we do that?" David asked.

"Revenue predictability is a function of Marketing Sophistication. When we see lumpy revenue, that's a sign marketing is underdeveloped. So, to solve your revenue problem, we're going to have to build a more sophisticated marketing function for ClearTrack."

UNDERSTANDING MARKETING SOPHISTICATION

If you were to put most organizations on a spectrum of marketing maturity, where the X-axis is the amount of budget they have and the Y-axis is how much pipeline marketing generates, most would fall closer to the underdeveloped extreme.

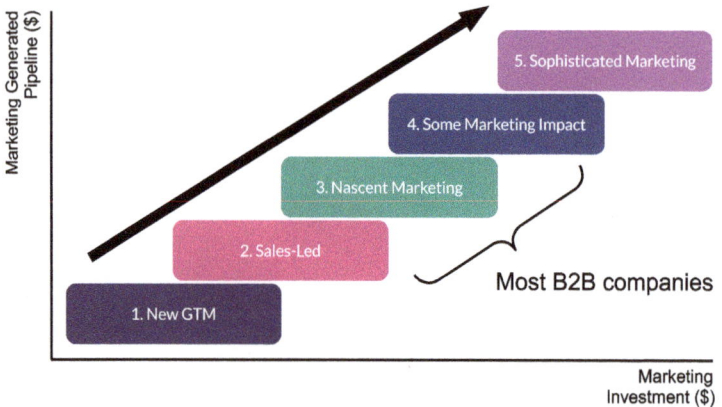

There are outliers, of course. Companies like Shopify, Atlassian, Monday, etc. have figured out the magic of marketing in helping them grow faster. Most companies, however, are nowhere close to that level of strategy, execution, or sophistication.

The more Marketing Generated Pipeline a company produces, the more mature it likely is. This is why Marketing Generated Pipeline is a good way to quickly map a company's Marketing Sophistication.

It's rare to find companies that have Marketing Generated Pipeline north of 50 percent. In Product-Led companies, this is more common, of course. But most B2B companies have Sales-Led motions, and Marketing Generated Pipeline is almost always below 25 percent in those instances.

Maturity Level	Pipeline Contribution	Team
New GTM	0%	0–1
Sales-Led	<10%	1–3
Nascent	10–15%	3–5
Some Marketing	15–25%	5–10
Sophisticated	25–50%+	10+

In ClearTrack's case, this number was only 15 percent.

This hardly surprised me. Whenever revenue is unpredictable, odds are Marketing is making a marginal impact.

"Isn't that a good thing?" David asked me. "We've grown to $7M without heavy marketing investment. Now they can grow this thing even more."

"That's not an unreasonable assumption," I responded. "But the more things investors like Pinnacle have to figure out to get the business to a healthy place, the less likely they are to close the transaction. It's like trying to sell a house that needs a lot of renovations to the kitchen or bathrooms. Buyers are just more resistant."

This is the dance that founders can't completely figure out, and understandably so. In most Sales-Led companies, Marketing is just not a priority. Every time there is more capital available to invest, the decision is always weighed against hiring another sales rep, and inevitably Sales gets the funding because it seems like the quickest path to closing more deals. Over time, a company can soar north of $10M without ever having more than three marketers or more than 15 percent Marketing Contribution to Pipeline.

The problem with this kind of thinking is that it eventually catches up. Closed Won Revenue is a function of how many opportunities are in the pipeline. Opportunities are a function of how many qualified and good-fit prospects enter the top of the funnel. And prospects are a function of how much we spend on marketing.

Relying on cold outbound with sales reps can get you to a certain level of growth, but eventually, the leads dry up and reps stop making quota. Most companies resort to ineffective strategies to resolve the problem of a missed quota. They throw money at expensive sales kickoffs every year, replace sales reps, change things like compensation structures and territory coverage, and even fire their VPs of Sales and Chief Revenue Officers.

Meanwhile, they never fix the underlying problem. How can we close more deals if we don't have more pipeline?

I asked David to pull up his pipeline coverage. David's goal for the year was to close $3M in new ARR. ClearTrack had only thirty SQLs and $750K in pipeline when he pulled up the report in Salesforce. No wonder their revenue generation was sporadic.

"This is what our coverage normally looks like," said David. "We add pipeline a lot slower than we close deals."

As we broke down the numbers further, here's what I learned about the ClearTrack business:

- The Average Deal Size for its ideal customers was $25,000
- Blended Customer Acquisition Cost (CAC) Payback Period was 7 months
- SQLs closed at a rate of 33 percent
- Demo to SQL rates were 25 percent
- Net Revenue Retention was 95 percent
- Lifetime Value (LTV) was hovering around 6 years
- Year-over-Year (YoY) growth was 15 percent
- Earnings before interest, taxes, depreciation, and amortization (EBITDA) margins were $700K or about 10 percent
- Cash on hand was about $1.2M

"We're going to need six to eight times that pipeline to improve your predictability," I told David as I walked him through the math behind my statement. "To close $3M in new ARR, ClearTrack needs at least 360 SQLs and $9M in pipeline (33 percent conversion) and 1,440 demos (25 percent conversion). And these numbers assume conversion rates will hold as more volume enters the funnel."

"That feels almost impossible given where we are as a business," said David, feeling overwhelmed by the task at hand.

"It's not as difficult as it seems," I said encouragingly. "ClearTrack has all the pieces needed to figure this out."

SCORECARDING YOUR MARKETING POTENTIAL

One thing founders underestimate is how strong their business fundamentals really are. The stronger the fundamentals, the more aggressively you should invest in your marketing.

KPI	1	2	3	4	5
CAC Payback (months)	>36 months	24–36 months	18–23 months	12–17 months	<12 months
Demo to Opp Rate (%)	<10%	10–19%	20–29%	30–39%	40%+
Opp to Close Rate (%)	<10%	10–19%	20–29%	30–39%	40%+
LTV (years)	<1 year	1–3 years	4–5 years	6–10 years	>10 years
NRR (%)	<80%	80–89%	90–94%	95–100%	>100%

If you were to take the previous scorecarding table and score a business out of 5 on each of the above factors, you'd come to a recommendation on how aggressive that business should be with their marketing investment. The higher the score, the better positioned a business is in their ability to invest in marketing.

Score	Ability to Scale	Direction
21–25	Excellent	Scale Marketing spend aggressively
16–20	Good	Scale Marketing spend aggressively
11–15	Average	Optimize Marketing spend
6–10	Below Average	Leverage Marketing to reduce waste and leaks
<5	Poor	Fix other areas before investing in Marketing

ClearTrack scored a 20 as per the numbers shared earlier:

KPI	Value	Score
Blended CAC Payback (months)	7 months	5
Demo to Opp Rate (%)	25%	3
Opp to Close Rate (%)	33%	4
LTV (years)	6 years	4
Net Revenue Retention (NRR) (%)	95%	4

"ClearTrack's fundamentals are strong," I explained to David. "It's how we know we can confidently invest in Marketing without worrying about returns."

This is one of the big things founders miss. As they build their business, they often err on the side of caution rather than aggression, even when the numbers dictate they should switch to another gear. It's easy to understand why founders do this. They're always balancing cash flow and limited resources against competing priorities.

In the process, founders leave a lot of money on the table without even realizing it. Each additional dollar of ARR is worth three to seven times in terms of enterprise value when exiting the business. In ClearTrack's case, with a blended CAC Payback Period of only 7 months, it could confidently invest $1 today and know that it would increase enterprise value by $5 in just half a year. Not only that, but with a blended CAC Payback Period of only 7 months, ClearTrack wouldn't have to worry about being strapped for cash on its marketing spend as future customers would fund its increased spend on Marketing.

As I explained this to David, he got far more comfortable. "Where do we start?" he asked.

"This is where we have to make sure all the right building blocks are in place before we scale," I answered.

PYRAMID OF MARKETING SOPHISTICATION

What ClearTrack needed to do was build a good story about its revenue potential. That story needed an underlying framework and process the company could follow to increase its Marketing Sophistication and overall Contribution to Pipeline.

A good way to think about building Marketing Sophistication is as a pyramid.

- **Layer 1 (Foundation):** This is where most of the groundwork of a mature marketing engine is laid.

- **Layer 2 (Programs):** Most of the actual value from marketing is created here by running programs and campaigns, and creating content.

- **Layer 3 (Resourcing):** This is where the right team and budget needs to be procured from the CEO and the board.

- **Layer 4 (Outcome):** The ultimate goal of driving revenue growth is a result of all the other layers of work.

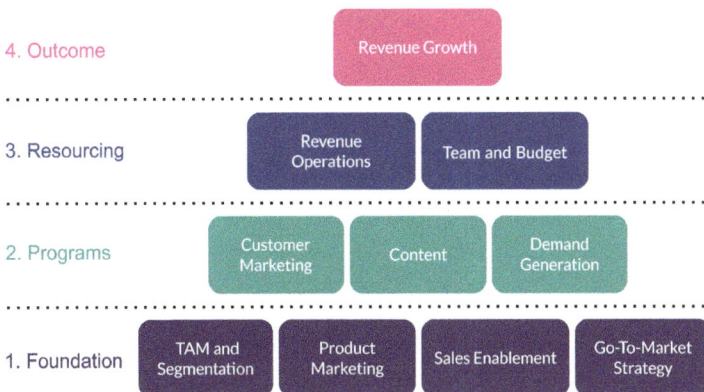

4. Outcome	Revenue Growth		
3. Resourcing	Revenue Operations	Team and Budget	
2. Programs	Customer Marketing	Content	Demand Generation
1. Foundation	TAM and Segmentation	Product Marketing	Sales Enablement	Go-To-Market Strategy

Each box in the pyramid represents a key area where the company needs to build sophistication. It's important to understand that sophistication does not imply being world class in that area. In a lot of founder-led businesses, the answer lies in getting to "good enough" so you can focus on driving revenue.

"Most companies I encounter do not have most of these boxes built out," I explained to David.

Every company wants the outcome of predictable revenue growth, but most have not done the fundamental work required. When we meet companies, they typically look more like the image below, which is quite close to what ClearTrack's pyramid looked like:

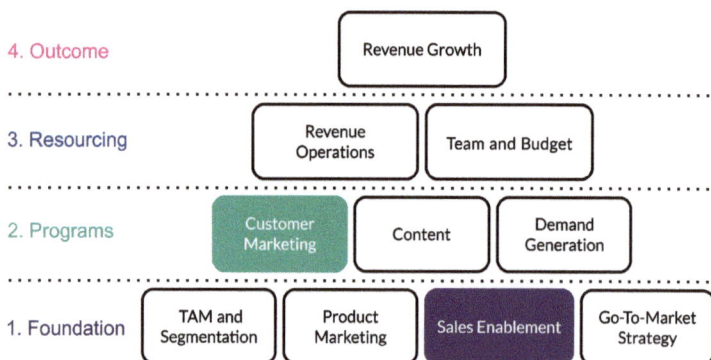

4. Outcome		Revenue Growth		
3. Resourcing		Revenue Operations	Team and Budget	
2. Programs	Customer Marketing	Content	Demand Generation	
1. Foundation	TAM and Segmentation	Product Marketing	Sales Enablement	Go-To-Market Strategy

These kinds of companies have usually done some Product Marketing work, have some content on their blog or website, and have some Marketing budget to fund their activities. However, most of them have not achieved a level of sophistication in most of the boxes because this work is often skipped for more near-term opportunities. For example, if there is a big trade show coming up, Marketing focuses all its resources on supporting that trade show and the Sales team that's attending. Meanwhile, the website is not set up to convert, there's no accountability framework in place for Marketing, and basic demand gen programs have not been launched.

Getting the order of operations right is critical here. You need to invest in all the boxes over time because that is how you increase Marketing Generated Pipeline and revenue predictably. The right order is to start at the bottom and work through each of the nine boxes one at a time.

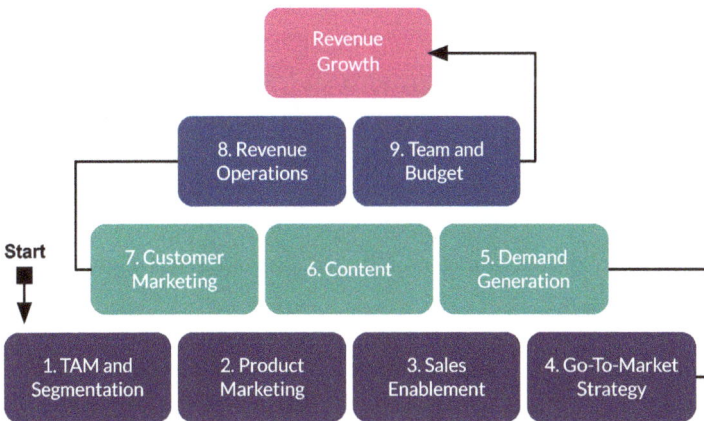

"Expecting Marketing to deliver pipeline and revenue without building out all these layers is like expecting Product-Market fit without talking to customers or developing new features or improving user experience," I continued to David. "This is the work we need to do together."

"I'm in. Let's do this," said David. He was bought in, which was a critical step. These kinds of transformations need buy-in from the CEO, who can push the agenda forward. It's their responsibility to rally the entire business around the initiative and make progress much faster than otherwise.

Over the next six months, I worked with David and his team to work through all the layers and increase ClearTrack's Marketing Sophistication. David had his team focused on making improvements and Marketing's Contribution to Pipeline and Revenue scaled consistently and predictably. ClearTrack also reached four times pipeline coverage while maintaining conversion rates and keeping its CAC Payback Period under 12 months.

Just a year later, David put ClearTrack back on the market with a far more predictable revenue engine as an asset. Not only did Pinnacle Capital re-enter a bid, but it also paid a significantly higher valuation.

In the chapters ahead, you'll learn about the framework I took David and ClearTrack through. Each chapter corresponds to one box in the pyramid. There are nine steps and nine chapters, one for each box in the pyramid that precedes the desired outcome of driving revenue growth. We'll break down how to achieve sophistication in each box while using David and ClearTrack as our governing example.

This is the same framework I've deployed as the CEO of How To SaaS with hundreds of other B2B technology and software companies in different markets, verticals, and industries. I've even used it myself as the CMO of Wild Apricot, which was eventually acquired by Rubicon Technology Partners in 2017 and flipped to Pamlico Capital in 2018.

It works. It will work for you too.

By the end of this book, you'll have an exact understanding of how to build a more sophisticated Marketing engine for your business so you are generating more pipeline and revenue than ever before.

You'll also increase your odds of being acquired and the likelihood of exiting your business at a significantly higher valuation.

1

TAM AND SEGMENTATION

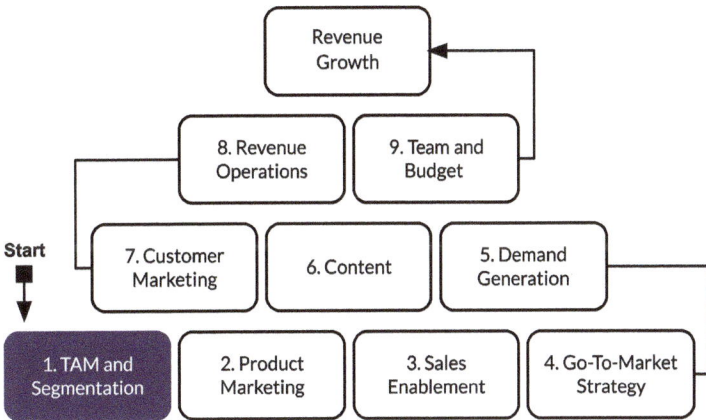

"Who is your ideal customer?" I asked David.

"Anyone who needs project management software," he responded.

This was the kind of response I was used to hearing from founders. Their Total Addressable Market (TAM) is in the billions of dollars, the number of targets are in the millions, and almost the entire market is greenfield.

Nothing could be further from the truth.

"Our solution is horizontal, you see," David continued. "Any market where project management is important is a good fit for our software."

"That might be true, but that doesn't mean you should go after them," I explained. "Odds are most of those potential customers are a bad fit for your software."

Understanding exactly who your software is for is critical. In trying to build a bigger business, a lot of founders end up trying to be everything to everyone, even though a smaller group of customers are really their biggest champions.

The key is to break down the customer data by segment, vertical, industry, size, and geography and compare them against each other using key performance indicators (KPIs) such as Demo to Opp rate, Opp to Close rates, NRR, and Net Promoter Score (NPS).

As we dug into the data for ClearTrack, a few patterns emerged. First, smaller accounts with less than five seats made up over 40 percent of ClearTrack's new demos every month. However, these accounts had really poor conversion and retention rates. Over 50

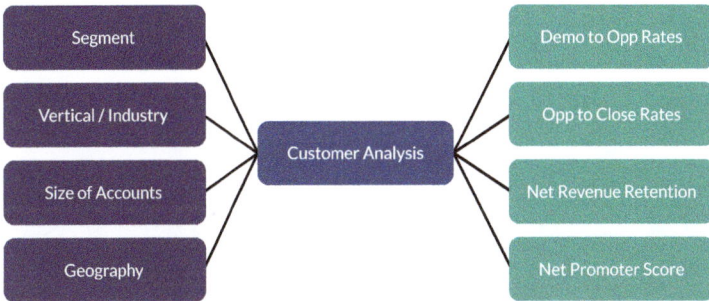

percent of them churned within the first 6 months. Second, certain industries where Project Management software should be mission critical like SaaS and Construction were not adopting the software at high rates. The SQL to Closed Won rate on these verticals was lower than 10 percent. Third, the NPS on all three groups with the software was below 0.

Meanwhile, other customers were wildly successful with the ClearTrack platform. These customers had certain characteristics:

- They had ten or more seats
- They were all Professional Services firms—Consulting, Engineering, Architecture, Lawyers, Accountants
- They all valued the time tracking features of ClearTrack, which made sense in the services verticals
- Their Net Retention Rates were 110 percent
- ClearTrack sat at the heart of their business operations, Project Management, workforce management, and invoicing
- Their collective NPS was forty-plus

"By figuring this out, we've already shifted the entire focus of the business," I said to David. "We now have a clear target to build our entire Go-To-Market around."

IDENTIFYING BEST-FIT CUSTOMERS

Analyzing existing customer data can reveal a whole lot about who you should go after. Your best-fit customers likely have the best metrics across the board.

Fit	Demo to Opp	Opp to Close Rates	NRR	NPS
High	35%+	40%+	100%+	Promoters (>30)
Medium	20–35%	25–40%	85–100%	Passives (0–30)
Low	<20%	<25%	<85%	Detractors (<0)

In ClearTrack's case, the customer data looked like this:

Vertical	Demo to Opp	Opp to Close	NRR	NPS
Engineering	45%	55%	120%	72
Architecture	40%	45%	110%	55
Consulting	35%	40%	105%	47
Legal	24%	33%	95%	23
Accounting	21%	28%	92%	18
Construction	15%	22%	85%	-7
SaaS	11%	15%	75%	-18
Micro (<5 seats)	22%	20%	50%	-30

Based on how these metrics measured up to our best-fit customer scorecard, we could assign each vertical an overall fit rating of high, medium, or low.

Looking at the data, the takeaways are obvious. Engineering, Architecture, and Consulting firms loved ClearTrack. Legal and Accounting firms were still promoters, though less of an ideal fit. Construction, SaaS, and Micro accounts were just a terrible fit for the product.

When looking at the market landscape of other solutions available to customers, these numbers made sense. Micro organizations can choose from all kinds of free and low-priced offerings like Trello, Asana, and Monday. SaaS companies have specific needs that platforms like Jira serve better. Construction companies have far more complex needs that purpose-built solutions like Procore serve better. Accounting and Legal platforms have industry-specific platforms like Netsuite, Xero, Clio, and MyCase, though they were still getting use out of the platform. However, Engineering, Architecture, and Consulting firms did not have a platform servicing their needs the way ClearTrack was.

"I can't believe this data has been sitting right under our noses the entire time," said David, shocked and disappointed.

"It's normal to not have done this work at the stage ClearTrack is at today," I said. "At least we know now."

UNCOVERING MARKET PENETRATION

One of the first things investors like Pinnacle Capital do during due diligence is customer and market analysis. They'll hire external firms to interview your biggest accounts, do mystery shopping, create their own case studies, and calculate independent NPS scores. What they are really trying to figure out is how to accurately size the market opportunity. The more convincing the market opportunity, the more interesting an investment becomes. Notice, by the way, that I said "more convincing" instead of "larger"—that's because the company needs to illustrate its ability to win a particular market over. This is where being specific is more important than being generic.

Instead of waiting for a future buyer to do this work, David and I decided to illustrate how big the potential TAM for ClearTrack really was. We took the top verticals and segments we identified and mapped the market opportunity.

Vertical	Customers	Total Market	Penetration
Engineering	95	14,500	0.7%
Architecture	67	7,500	0.9%
Consulting	52	67,000	0.1%
Legal	44	36,000	0.1%
Accounting	29	25,000	0.1%

Across the board, ClearTrack's market penetration for its ideal-fit customers was less than 1 percent. Given that Micro accounts had higher churn rates, we segmented out accounts with more than ten seats in the same verticals.

Vertical	Customers (>10 seats)	Large Accounts (>10 seats)	Penetration
Engineering	45	4,200	1.1%
Architecture	39	1,200	3.3%
Consulting	31	12,500	0.2%
Legal	28	5,700	0.5%
Accounting	17	3,100	0.5%

With both filters applied, ClearTrack's TAM still had 26,700 ideal targets, with a market penetration of less than 4 percent in each vertical. What's more is that most of these firms were not on a competitor solution. About 85 percent of the market was a true greenfield opportunity, meaning there were at least 22,695 untouched targets available to be captured.

UNDERSTANDING CONVERSION RATES

When David and I sat down with Bryan, ClearTrack's VP of Sales, to show him what we had uncovered, he let out a sigh of relief. He had known from the front lines that they weren't setting demos with the best prospects.

"I've been saying for a while now that most of the leads Marketing has been sending us are not good fit leads," said Bryan. "Every time I've brought it up, Katie and the Marketing team defend it by saying we're not closing the deals as well as we should be."

David had found himself caught in between this battle for almost a year. Katie, his VP of Marketing, would insist that they were doing good work. She would bring data on the number of leads and demos the Marketing team was bringing in every month while showing how win rates (the rate at which opportunities close) were stagnant or declining. This always put the onus on Bryan and the Sales team to defend why deals weren't closing.

I sat with Katie to get a month-by-month breakdown of demos booked for the previous two years. Here is what we found:

Verticals and Segments	Avg. Demos per Month	Demo to Opp	Opp to Close
Engineering	5	45%	55%
Architecture	7	40%	45%
Consulting	4	35%	40%
Legal	3	24%	33%
Accounting	2	21%	28%
Construction	3	15%	22%
SaaS	10	11%	15%
Micro (<5 seats)	22	22%	20%

Despite being the lowest converting verticals across the board, Micro, SaaS, and Construction leads made up nearly 65 percent of the volume Marketing was bringing in.

In trying to be everything to everyone, ClearTrack's Go-To-Market was way too broad. It was reeling in prospects from so many bad-fit segments and verticals, which was taking focus away from the good-fit customers. The sales team was spending too much time trying to close bad-fit deals, while win rates were declining. And the Marketing team was investing in programs that were bringing in too many of the bad-fit prospects into the funnel.

Bryan felt vindicated. No wonder he and the Sales team were complaining. Until now, David just didn't have the right framework to referee the ongoing battle between Sales and Marketing. To Katie's credit, she didn't argue with the data. She was ready to figure out how to move forward together to achieve a common objective.

"We need to change who we are going after," said David as he looked at the data. "We need to rally the whole team around our ideal customers from this point forward."

By having an exactly defined universe of targets, not only had we solved a major internal battle, but we also focused the entire team around an exact target of ideal customers. We could now get Katie and the Marketing team to tell a better story about ClearTrack to the market.

2

PRODUCT MARKETING

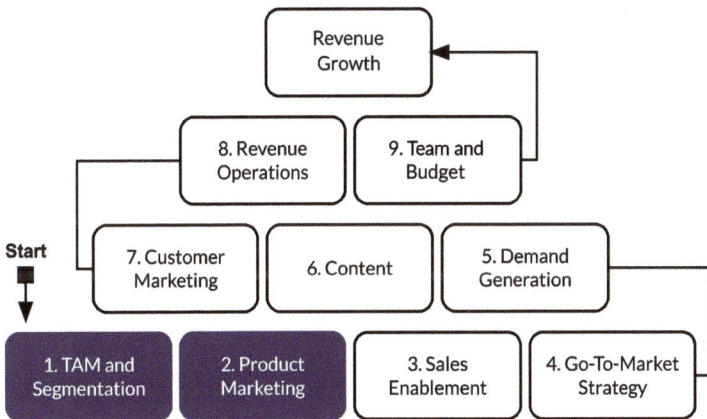

"Don't we risk losing potential customers if we say we're only focused on a limited number of verticals?" David asked me.

"Yes, you do," I answered. "And that's a good thing."

Even though we had gone through the exercise of defining ClearTrack's best-fit customers, David had the understandable fear of turning away good business. After all, what if a large construction company came to the website and saw messaging focused only on Professional Services firms?

This is where a founder's resolve is really tested. Once you create a rigid demarcation between who is your ideal customer and who isn't, you end up turning away a lot more business than you're comfortable with. That's painful for founders, who were often the first salesperson in the company.

One of the most common ways in which companies get distracted is when there is a deal on the table and revenue hanging in the balance. When this happens in the early days, founders distract the business in the interest of cash flow by taking on customers who aren't an ideal fit. As time goes on, sales reps continue this tradition and ask for features, discounts, and anything else it will take to close the deal. If there are not strict guidelines in place for what is an acceptable concession to close a deal, strategy goes out the window.

This is where Product Marketing's role in the process is amplified. We must outline exactly who we are going after, what we are going to say to them and why they should pick us over other options. The return on this work is infinite because it impacts all aspects of the business. As we get better at targeting our ideal customers, overall funnel efficiency improves; gross margins go up; win rates, LTV, and NRR dramatically improve; and customers are happier and refer more business.

```
                    ┌─────────────────────┐
                    │  Product Marketing  │
                    └─────────────────────┘
```

1. Improved Funnel Efficiency	2. Better Gross Margins	3. Higher Win Rates, LTV, NRR	4. More Referrals, Higher NPS

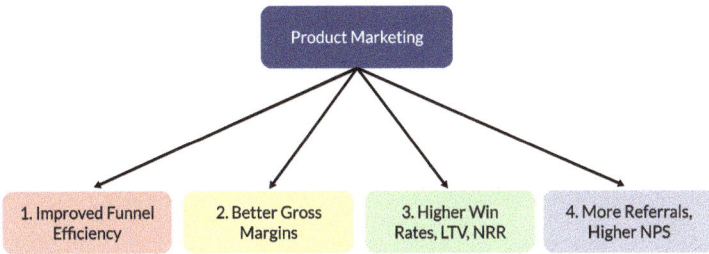

As a company builds a more focused Messaging, Positioning, and Go-To-Market, the lost revenue from bad-fit customers is more than made up by the increased volume and revenue from its best-fit customers. This trade-off isn't visible initially because you have to say no to revenue before you land more of your best-fit customers. That's why founders get uncomfortable.

"You'll see a lift in revenue soon enough," I reassured David. "Let's see this process through."

We had already completed the first critical step of the Product Marketing process: identifying our winning segments and verticals. We now had to translate that into Product Marketing to communicate that to the market.

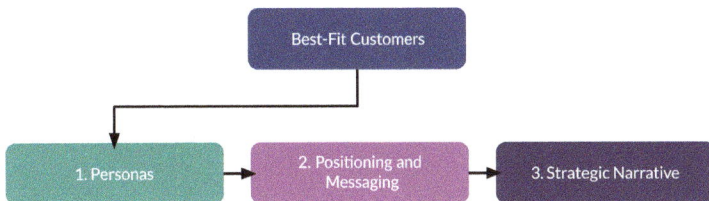

```
                    ┌─────────────────────┐
                    │  Best-Fit Customers │
                    └─────────────────────┘
```

1. Personas	→	2. Positioning and Messaging	→	3. Strategic Narrative

"We need to solve for three key persona types," I explained to David. "The buyer, the influencer, and the user."

The reason this was important is that companies often underestimate how many parties are involved when making a purchasing decision. The buyer is the one who controls the budget and is the ultimate decision-maker. The influencer gets to make an input into the decision as they are affected by the outcome. The user is the person who utilizes the solution at the end of the buying process. In some cases, these three people are effectively one individual. In others, there can be several people involved who each fit into one or more of the buckets. The key is to speak to each persona type so each understands the core benefits to themselves in their respective roles.

"Those are often distinct roles inside the best-fit segments we identified," said David. "The buyer is often the CEO or COO. The influencer is usually the Office Manager or CFO. The user is the person providing the professional service."

"Great," I said, impressed with how specific David's answers were. "We need to spell out exactly what each of these people cares about."

UPDATING PERSONAS

I collaborated with David, Katie, and Bryan to completely revamp their old Product Marketing work. We started by mapping out basic personas for each of the profiles David had identified to help us understand exactly who we were going after.

We outlined the overall mindset, goals, challenges, and objections ClearTrack would face with each of these stakeholders and had both the Sales and Marketing teams provide feedback to improve the profiles. Having all parties in the room contributing to a unified persona definition is an exercise David had never done with his team before. *(Note: These profiles have been simplified for our purposes here.)*

CEOs and COOs (Buyers)	
Mindset	To build a better Professional Services business
Goals / Drivers	• Increase efficiency in servicing clients • Improve quality of experience for clients • Manage workload and capacity versus hiring
Challenges	• Lack of visibility into service team productivity • Unable to track KPIs on service team efficiency • Difficult to figure out current team's capacity to service clients
Objections	• Adopting a new solution will take too much time and effort • Too big of a learning curve for team members • Too expensive

CFOs (Influencers)	
Mindset	To enhance the overall financial processes for the business
Goals/ Drivers	• Clearer visibility into billable hours and gross margins on projects • Improved forecasting and budgeting • Better cash flow management
Challenges	• Lack of transparency into time tracking and service team capacity • Difficulty making decisions related to hiring • Delayed invoicing and backlogged Accounts Receivable
Objections	• Must integrate with existing accounting system • Cannot be too complicated for junior finance team members to use

Service Team (Users)	
Mindset	To deliver projects successfully
Goals/ Drivers	• Stay on top of tasks and milestones • Improve quality of experience with clients • Manage competing priorities and projects
Challenges	• Managing manual processes • Communicating progress across projects within the organization
Objections	• Must not add too much admin work to the existing process • Must be easy to use

"It's funny," said David. "Until now, we've only talked about our buyers in the realm of project management. This is the first time we've looked at their needs as Professional Services firms."

I nodded. "Understanding your best-fit customers has a way of changing how everyone looks at the business."

David was finally seeing how our work could increase the impact of his entire Go-To-Market. He was more bought in now than he was when we started the process.

CREATING NEW POSITIONING AND MESSAGING

With the newfound clarity around who we were going after, it was time to nail down exactly what key points we wanted to drive home with our ideal customers.

"Positioning and Messaging work is critical here," I explained to David. "Right now, ClearTrack is communicating the benefits of project management software to everyone. We need to shift to communicating the benefits to Professional Services firms."

The first step was understanding the needs of ClearTrack's best-fit customers. These needs extended beyond what we had outlined for each of the more general personas because each type of firm had different challenges and constraints.

Top Verticals (Engineering, Architecture, Consulting, Legal, Accounting)	
Stated Needs	**Unstated Needs**
Creating and managing unique projects with different tasks, milestones, and stakeholders	Having a flexible system that is easy to use
Building better project estimates to prevent going over budget	Having better financial predictability and being more profitable
Better time tracking and resource planning	Having a more transparent way to manage productivity and maximize utilization
Staying on top of billable hours and invoicing	Having Accounts Receivable paid on time and better cash flow

"What they need is so different from what we've been saying to the market," noticed David.

ClearTrack was spending so much energy on trying to sound like another Project Management software company that it had completely ignored what its biggest fans really needed and why they loved the product. When compared with ClearTrack's legacy positioning, you can see how stark the contrast in focus really is.

	Old	New
Ideal Customers	Any company needing Project Management software	Professional Services firms (Engineering, Architecture, Consulting, Legal, and Accounting)
Problem	Managing any project, large or small.	Building the underlying framework for managing complex Professional Services engagements.
Relevant Features	• Project and Task Management • Kanban Boards • Project Templates • Status Updates	• Project and Task Management • Time Tracking and Invoicing • Resource Planning • Budgeting and Forecasting
Competitors	Trello, Asana, Monday, Jira	BigTime, Kantata

The old approach had ClearTrack focused on an entirely different market with a different set of competitors. How could it compete with market leaders like Trello, Asana, Monday, and Jira when its product was not built for the same kinds of customers? It was a losing battle.

If we ran a feature-by-feature comparison, it would have been easy to see that the competing platforms were able to offer significantly more value than ClearTrack as a standalone Project

Management software. Those platforms simply had way more resources and funding to compete in the ultra-competitive market of Project Management. As a result, ClearTrack's Right to Win (the likelihood of a customer choosing ClearTrack over any of their competitors) in this market was not compelling enough to be a legitimate threat.

Project Management	Trello	Asana	Monday	Jira
Right to Win	Low	Medium	Low	Medium

Conversely, the new approach had ClearTrack focused on best-fit customers, in the right market, against the right competitors. ClearTrack's product had a Right to Win in this market, and its functionality superseded the other options like BigTime and Kantata.

Professional Services	BigTime	Kantata	Trello	Asana	Monday	Jira
Right to Win	High	High	High	Medium	High	High

In taking the new approach, ClearTrack had also removed the threat of competition from the Project Management space as it also had a Right to Win over those platforms in the Professional Services market.

"Now that we understand our positioning in this space, we can focus on communicating why customers should choose ClearTrack over other competitors," I said to David.

Messaging Framework	
Solution Overview	ClearTrack provides Professional Services firms with an underlying framework to run all business operations: • Client Engagements and Projects • Resource Planning, Time Tracking, and Workforce Management • Budgeting, Forecasting, and Financial Management
Key Benefits	• Track complex and unique client projects in one place • Build standardized processes and workflows to improve efficiency • Maximize utilization with full visibility into team workload and bandwidth • Track billable hours and invoice faster • Improve cash flow management with better understanding of project profitability
Why ClearTrack	• Purpose-built for Professional Services firms • End-to-end operating system connecting Sales, Client Services, and Finance • Data-driven visibility to optimize and streamline all business operations • Central source of truth for the entire business

"Wow," said David. "I can't believe how much better this sounds than what we've been communicating to the market."

Katie and Bryan echoed the sentiment. David, Katie, Bryan, and I had built this framework together, leveraging customer data, insights, and analysis from Sales and Marketing sources to get it to this point. Just the act of doing this exercise as a group brought the team closer together. The tension between Katie and Bryan seemed to have dissipated. They were on the same team now.

"I guess I should get my team working to distribute this message right away," said Katie.

"Not yet," I said. "There's one more critical step we cannot skip."

BUILDING A STRATEGIC NARRATIVE

The critical step I was referring to was the same step almost all software companies miss.

Regardless of how much customer analysis, segmentation, positioning, and messaging work is done, eventually companies find themselves targeting a set of customers in a known market or category. It is rare to be the only provider in a category. The only occasions where this happens is when a company is actually creating the category. In most other instances, there are at least one or two other providers that customers can choose instead of your platform.

This is where feature parity is the enemy. Over time, most companies end up having a similar feature set, and customers are left with a commoditized choice. When this happens, the only way to compete is to race to the bottom on pricing. While a scary notion, this is the reality of most software companies that have an undifferentiated brand in the marketplace. It's also one of the primary reasons why most of them do not grow as fast as the leaders in a particular category.

"We need to elevate the conversation away from features," I explained to David. "This is not just about running a better Professional Services firm."

"And how do we do that?" David asked, playing along.

"By building a Strategic Narrative," I explained. "We need to show the market that ClearTrack is the difference between them winning and losing."

It was a hard concept to digest.

The reason people pick one product over another is they believe it aligns most closely with their values and who they want to become. ClearTrack needed to tell the Professional Services market a better story for why its software mattered.

This meant shifting the focus away from features and benefits and moving it toward something far more aspirational: how those customers saw themselves and their businesses evolving over time. The way to do that was to highlight how customers could grow their Professional Services firm faster if they had ClearTrack at the heart of their operations versus if they continued operating the way they currently were.

	Before ClearTrack	After ClearTrack
Day-to-Day Reality	Overwhelmed with day-to-day operations, organizing projects, and managing people.	Streamlined operating system for the entire business.
Insights	Not enough visibility into profitability, performance, cash flow, or utilization.	Full transparency and visibility into the overall performance and financial metrics of the firm.
Priorities	Keeping the trains running on time, ensuring projects are being delivered.	Peace of mind in knowing the service team is delivering, turning focus to generating more revenue.
Outcomes	Not enough sophistication as a Professional Services firm, stagnant revenue.	High degree of sophistication, with growing revenue and profitability.

By elevating the conversation to this level, ClearTrack could now speak to its ideal customers' visions for their respective businesses. This created a messaging waterfall for our ideal customers.

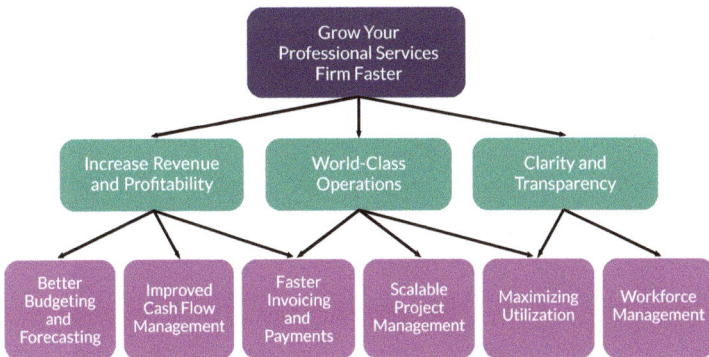

The brand promise was that if you were serious about growing your Professional Services firm, you needed to use ClearTrack. It would help you grow faster, improve your operations, give you clarity and transparency into performance, and help you increase revenue and profitability. ClearTrack was purpose-built to get Professional Services firms from here to where they wanted to go.

All of this was done without ever mentioning a single feature. That was the magic of a powerful Strategic Narrative.

David's eyes lit up. "This is what you mean by elevating the conversation."

"Exactly," I responded. "We're not just selling features and benefits. We are selling a transformation."

We were now ready to communicate our new message to the market.

3

SALES ENABLEMENT

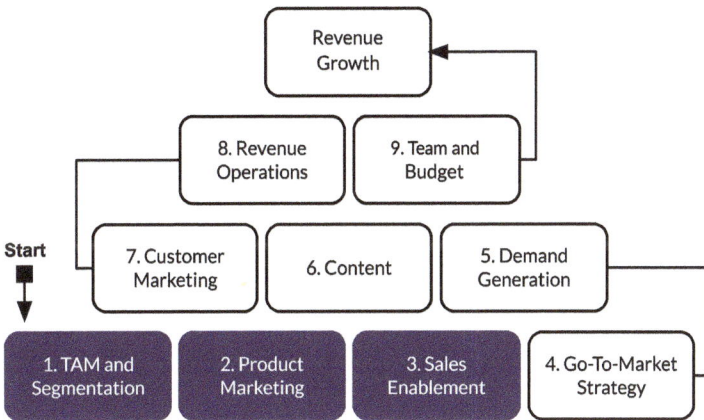

"Overhauling the website and all sales enablement materials feels like a big project that will take too long," said David. "Aren't we already converting our top verticals at high win rates?"

David was right. As a refresher from the first chapter, here are the conversion rates on ClearTrack's top verticals.

Verticals and Segments	Avg. Demos per Month	Demo to Opp	Opp to Close
Engineering	5	45%	55%
Architecture	7	40%	45%
Consulting	4	35%	40%
Legal	3	24%	33%
Accounting	2	21%	28%
Construction	3	15%	22%
SaaS	10	11%	15%
Micro (<5 seats)	22	22%	20%

"It's impressive that your close rates for ideal customers have been so high even though your messaging doesn't target them specifically," I responded. "But that's exactly why they're considered ideal customers."

The problem wasn't that the ideal customers weren't converting. The problem was finding more of them. If you recall, ClearTrack's market penetration across its top verticals was less than 1 percent.

Vertical	Customers	Total Market	Penetration
Engineering	95	14,500	0.7%
Architecture	67	7,500	0.9%
Consulting	52	67,000	0.1%
Legal	44	36,000	0.1%
Accounting	29	25,000	0.1%

When ideal customers found their way into ClearTrack's funnel, they converted at high rates. There just weren't enough of them finding their way into the funnel.

As it stood, ClearTrack was only averaging twenty-one demos per month from its ideal customers. Factoring in its conversion rates at every stage, this meant ClearTrack was closing three deals per month on average from its top verticals.

"We're just not getting enough at-bats with our best-fit customers," I explained to David.

This was the pipeline ClearTrack needed to hit their targets:

	New ARR	Deals	Opps	Demos
Annual	$3,000,000	120	360	1,440
Monthly	$250,000	10	30	120

"We need to meet six times as many of our ideal-fit customers every month," I reminded David as I pulled up the projections we needed to hit. "We should be holding 120 demos per month with them in order to hit the 1,440 demos we need annually to close $3 million in new ARR."

This is where the value of Sales Enablement work comes in. One of the most common misconceptions about Sales Enablement content is that it is limited to sales materials and scripts that reps use to sell to prospects. In a world where information is everywhere, Sales Enablement is about any piece of content that a potential customer can find and learn more about your business.

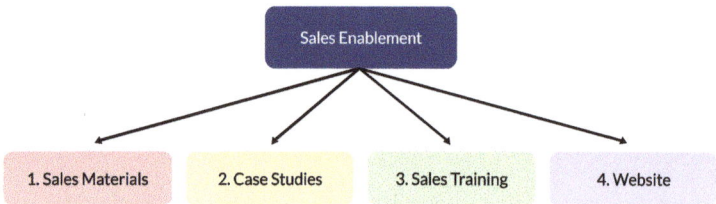

Sales Enablement is:

1. Any sales materials (sales decks, battle cards, objection handling documents) that the sales team uses to talk to customers
2. Case studies that showcase the success current customers have had with the platform
3. All sales training used to get new and existing reps ramped up to have sales conversations with prospects and customers
4. The website where prospects and customers can self-serve and educate themselves through all stages of the sales process

This was the reason things needed to be overhauled. ClearTrack needed to go all in on its new segmentation, positioning, and messaging. Based on the work we had done in those areas, almost all of ClearTrack's Sales Enablement assets were outdated, and updating those assets was going to take time.

Founders like David get nervous when they consider the time involved and the lag between producing the assets and seeing their impact. They're constantly thinking about cash flow and fundraising. They want leads, pipeline, and revenue as soon as possible. Sometimes, this short-term thinking leads to less than ideal outcomes.

"By front-loading this work, we are setting up ClearTrack to have long-term growth," I impressed upon David. "It will pay off in a big way when we meet more of our best-fit customers."

This work needed to be done one way or another, and David understood that. Finding a shortcut was impossible. And the sooner it was done, the faster we'd get to increased pipeline and revenue.

IDENTIFYING REQUIRED SALES MATERIALS

Bryan pulled all their Sales Enablement materials. "Almost all our sales materials are focused around project management," he said.

As we looked through the materials together, I noticed a bunch of things that were off:

- None of the assets talked about ClearTrack as a purpose-built solution for Professional Service.
- There were no battle cards against competitors in the Professional Services software market.
- Sales-training or objection-handling documents that addressed the fears, uncertainties, and doubts of Professional Services firms were nonexistent.

There also wasn't any verticalized content for the best-fit customers we had identified. The assets that did exist talked about how ClearTrack solved the problem of Project Management for all companies.

"We need to flip this around entirely," I said. "We need our sales process to connect directly to the kinds of customers we want to land."

Each vertical needed its own sales deck, sales scripts, battle cards, and objection-handling documents. I mapped out exactly how many assets ClearTrack needed to produce.

Verticals and Segments	Sales Deck	Sales Scripts	Battle Cards	Objection Handling	Email Cadence
Engineering	5	10	5	10	10
Architecture	5	10	5	10	10
Consulting	5	10	5	10	10
Legal	5	10	5	10	10
Accounting	5	10	5	10	10

"Why do we need so many versions of each of these documents?" Bryan asked.

"It's not as many as it seems. There will be a lot of overlap," I explained. "But we need slightly different versions for each persona we identified, along with different versions for different sizes of accounts, large and small."

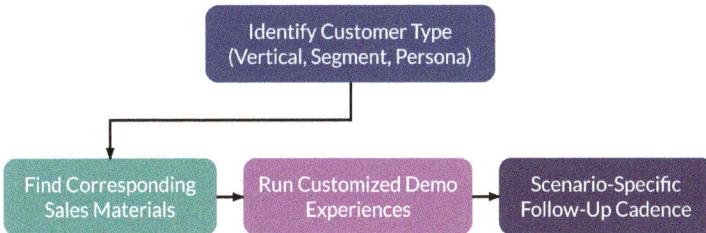

Identify Customer Type (Vertical, Segment, Persona)

Find Corresponding Sales Materials → Run Customized Demo Experiences → Scenario-Specific Follow-Up Cadence

By taking the same template for each piece of content and then adding minor customizations for each vertical, segment, and persona, Katie and Bryan got over 200 variations built out in less than a month.

We could now make the selling process foolproof. Content was how we were going to do that, especially as the sales team started to meet more of our ideal-fit customers.

BUILDING CASE STUDIES

I continued to look through ClearTrack's current content library to see how many case studies it had for each of our top verticals:

Vertical	Customers	NPS	Case Studies
Engineering	95	72	0
Architecture	67	55	1
Consulting	52	47	0
Legal	44	23	1
Accounting	29	18	1

Despite having glowing NPS scores, ClearTrack only had three case studies from its top verticals. Not only that, but ClearTrack published those case studies almost four years ago.

"More than anything, we need to showcase our ideal customers as the heroes we serve," I explained to Katie. "That's our starting point."

Highlighting the success stories of its best-fit customers was the best way to show future customers what kind of success they could achieve with the ClearTrack platform. ClearTrack simply did not have enough materials to showcase how it delivered on its brand promise to current customers.

It also gave ClearTrack a unique opportunity to emerge as a thought leader to Professional Services firms on how to build a bigger practice.

"I want at least three case studies for every one of our top verticals," I said to Katie. "One small customer, one mid-sized account, and one large account. We also need three case studies for each persona we identified. That will give us a case study for the full spectrum of prospects we encounter."

Over the next month, I had Katie and her team line up interviews with the highest NPS customers from each of the top verticals and create detailed case studies with answers to questions like:

- What was your reality before ClearTrack? What problems were you facing?
- What were you looking for in a solution?
- How did you find ClearTrack? How did you know it could help you solve those problems?
- How have you incorporated ClearTrack into your day-to-day operations?
- How much of an impact has ClearTrack made on your business?

- How much has your business grown since you started using ClearTrack?
- How much time/money has ClearTrack saved you?
- How has ClearTrack made your life better?

We recorded all the interviews on video, posted them on YouTube with transcriptions, repurposed them into articles and downloadable PDFs for the Sales team, and spliced them into smaller pieces of content. By the end of the process, ClearTrack had finished twenty-four full case studies with an additional ninety-six pieces of micro content to leverage across different channels to educate potential customers.

"We have to continue building this library," I told Katie, congratulating her on the great work the team had accomplished. "Every time we have a great customer story, we need to run it through this process. The content will serve the business forever."

Case studies are critical because they provide the social proof needed to drive a point home to potential customers. There is an inertia in every sale process because prospects always have the "do nothing" option available to them. If the pain point they're trying to solve is big enough, most customers search for a low-risk option to ease that pain.

Customers want to believe you have the antidote to their problems because it would be their quickest path to resolving something that has been a thorn in their side for far too long. This is where segmentation, Product Marketing, and Sales Enablement all come together to tell a unified story.

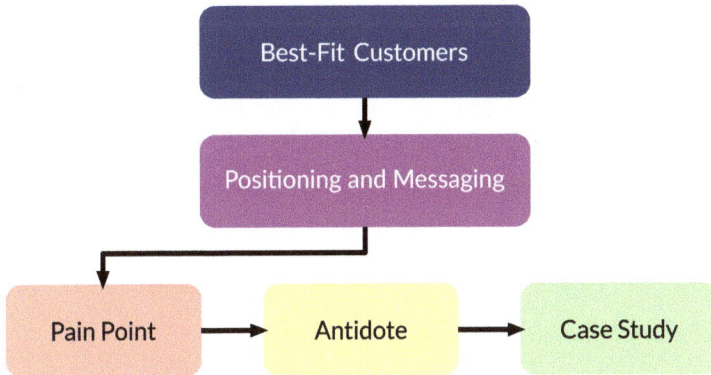

The reason for doing all this work is so that when a customer finally talks to a sales rep, the right frame for the conversation is set. This is where educating the Sales team on the exact focus of the business is critical.

TRAINING THE SALES TEAM

"Sales reps are one of the most important resources for buyers to educate themselves," I said to Katie. "If you don't educate the sales reps the right way, they won't educate buyers the right way."

ClearTrack's old framework had reps trying to overcome objections from customers comparing it to Asana and Monday when they weren't the right comparables at all. Reps were constantly running into conversations they couldn't win with prospects who weren't the best fit. When the wrong-fit customers fill the pipeline, the wrong Sales Enablement assets get created to overcome the wrong objections.

The role of the sales rep is not to convince the customer to buy a product that is not an ideal fit for them. Instead, it's to educate buyers on how to figure out what the right solution is for them based on who they are. Because we were changing who we were going after, ClearTrack needed a new way to educate buyers. This meant training reps on the adjusted focus.

Most companies underinvest in Sales Training. Everyone understands how important sales reps are to achieving revenue targets, yet very few companies give reps the requisite training needed to succeed. The SDR function is almost like a turnstile. Reps come in, stay for six months, and then most are let go. In market downturns, the first rounds of layoffs usually include batches of SDRs. What companies miss is that it is not enough to just give reps a chair, a new computer, and a phone against a list of prospects to call on and qualify.

The best sales reps have a deep understanding of the market, the Ideal Customer Profiles (ICPs), and the best-fit customers for a particular product. They know their dreams, their pain points, and what keeps them up at night. They understand what problems they are trying to solve and know how to address those problems with the solutions at their disposal. They are true market experts.

When companies first start, the founder is often the first salesperson. Naturally, the founder's knowledge and expertise about a particular market is just so high that close rates can often be higher than 50 percent. As companies scale and sales reps take over those functions, conversion rates plummet because the reps don't have nearly the same amount of market understanding.

How can we expect to hire inexperienced sales reps to be market experts if we don't invest in training them?

"What kind of training resources do we have for reps right now?" I asked Katie and Bryan.

"We do about a couple of days' worth of general onboarding," answered Bryan. "Then they use the general sales enablement assets we've got, and we train them as we go."

"I'd like to change that," I said to Bryan. "I'd like to set up a formalized training process for all sales reps to go through."

"Won't that take a huge investment to set up?" asked Bryan, worried about all the upfront work it would take to do this.

"Yes, it will," I said. "But it will pay off exponentially as we scale."

Inside most companies, the creation of this training content is owned by no one. Sales teams focus on sales activities and meeting quotas, while Marketing teams focus on generating more leads. In some larger companies, there are people in the role of Sales Enablement Managers, but it's not as common as one would think.

In ClearTrack, no one owned this domain.

"The Marketing team needs to own this for now," I explained to Katie and Bryan. "Sales training is essentially a content generation function, which includes project managing stakeholders who contribute that content. As we scale, we can always offload this back to Sales."

Over the next quarter, I worked with Katie's team to organize and structure a two-week Sales Training and Onboarding program for all reps, new and existing, to go through. The focus of the program was to help the reps understand:

1. The market of Engineering, Architecture, and Consulting firms
2. The updated ICPs, their realities, pain points, goals, and fears
3. The competitive landscape for ClearTrack in this market, what alternatives were available to the ICPs, and why ClearTrack was better for each segment

4. The full sales suitcase created by Marketing to enable the sales reps—decks, case studies, battle cards—so they knew where to find what they needed to close deals

As we continued to work through the process, the result was a Demo to Close rate north of 50 percent for all the top verticals identified as we scaled volumes.

Now that we had enabled the sales reps, we needed to enable the buyers with the ability to self-serve. The way to do that was by having the right content on the website.

UPDATING THE WEBSITE

"We've been primarily focused on SEO as a way to figure out what website content we need to create," said Katie.

While this was not the worst idea, it was misguided. ClearTrack didn't have any of the foundational content it needed on its website to communicate its value to best-fit customers. By focusing on SEO as the primary driver, all Katie had done was drive traffic from less-ideal customers. If you recall from Chapter 1, nearly 65 percent of ClearTrack's demos every month were from bad-fit verticals.

The website is the most precious asset for Product Marketing and Sales Enablement content. Every day, countless prospects and customers self-serve their way through all kinds of pages and content without ever interacting with a sales rep. This is prime real estate, and it should be treated as such. There is a hierarchy for prioritizing website content, with Product Marketing and Sales Enablement taking precedence.

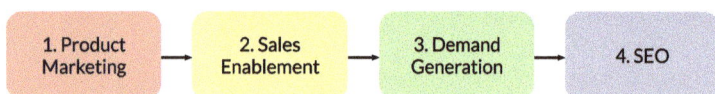

| 1. Product Marketing | → | 2. Sales Enablement | → | 3. Demand Generation | → | 4. SEO |

Prioritizing website content according to SEO when your Product Marketing is off is like trying to do the dishes while the house is on fire. You may feel like you're being productive, but you won't have a place to put those dishes very soon.

In ClearTrack's case, there were a few key website changes that needed to be made:

- The homepage made no references to its new positioning and messaging
- There were no dedicated pages for its identified best-fit customers, personas, or top verticals
- None of the Sales Enablement materials, particularly the case studies, were showcased

I sat down with Katie and walked her through all the assets we needed to support our updated Product Marketing work.

Web Page	Page Type	Requirements
Home Page	Landing Page	• Update with new messaging and positioning • Highlight top verticals and ideal customers • Add benefits and features related to best-fit customers
Engineering	Industries	• Dedicated page for Engineering firms • Highlight benefits and features related to Engineering firms • Showcase case studies of successful Engineering firms
Architecture	Industries	• Dedicated page for Architecture firms • Highlight benefits and features related to Architecture firms • Showcase case studies of successful Architecture firms
Consulting	Industries	• Dedicated page for Consulting firms • Highlight benefits and features related to Consulting firms • Showcase case studies of successful Consulting firms
Legal	Industries	• Dedicated page for Legal firms • Highlight benefits and features related to Legal firms • Showcase case studies of successful Legal firms
Accounting	Industries	• Dedicated page for Accounting firms • Highlight benefits and features related to Accounting firms • Showcase case studies of successful Accounting firms
CEOs	Solutions	• Dedicated page for CEOs • Highlight benefits and features related to CEOs • Showcase case studies of CEOs succeeding with ClearTrack
COOs	Solutions	• Dedicated page for COOs • Highlight benefits and features related to COOs • Showcase case studies of COOs succeeding with ClearTrack

Web Page	Page Type	Requirements
CFOs	Solutions	• Dedicated page for CFOs • Highlight benefits and features related to CFOs • Showcase case studies of CFOs succeeding with ClearTrack
Client Services	Solutions	• Dedicated page for Client Services • Highlight benefits and features related to Client Services • Showcase case studies of Client Services members succeeding with ClearTrack
Case Studies	Customers	• Showcase all case studies • Ability to filter case studies by vertical, segment, and persona
Time Tracking	Features	• Highlight value of time tracking in helping Professional Services firms scale • Showcase value to top verticals and personas
Resource Planning	Features	• Highlight value of resource planning in helping Professional Services firms scale • Showcase value to top verticals and personas
Budget and Forecasting	Features	• Highlight value of Budget and Forecasting in helping Professional Services firms scale • Showcase value to top verticals and personas
Billing and Invoicing	Features	• Highlight value of Billing and Invoicing in helping Professional Services firms scale • Showcase value to top verticals and personas
Project Management	Features	• Highlight value of Project Management in helping Professional Services firms scale • Showcase value to top verticals and personas

None of these pages, outside of the Project Management features page and the Homepage, currently existed on the ClearTrack website. Even those two pages had all the wrong messaging. All the new pages cumulated into an updated structure for the entire website.

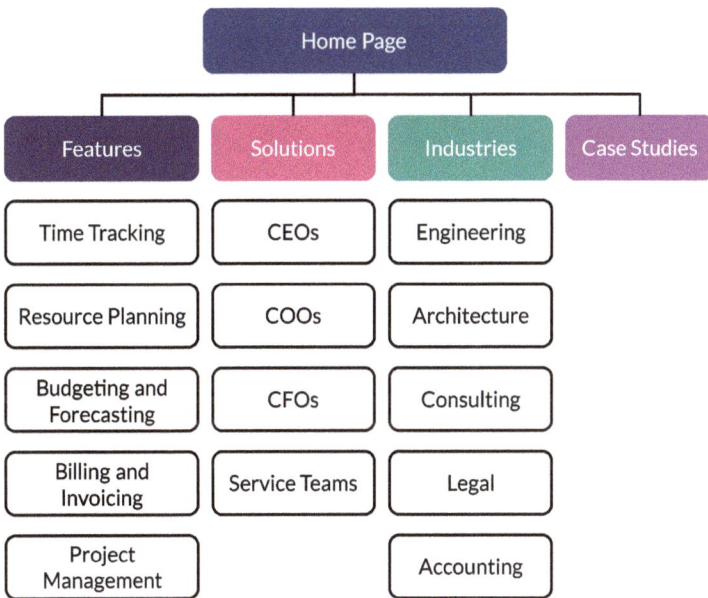

Home Page			
Features	**Solutions**	**Industries**	**Case Studies**
Time Tracking	CEOs	Engineering	
Resource Planning	COOs	Architecture	
Budgeting and Forecasting	CFOs	Consulting	
Billing and Invoicing	Service Teams	Legal	
Project Management		Accounting	

With a clear roadmap for what needed to be built, Katie and her team got to work to produce all the content required. This was the longest part of the content process but also the most important. What we build here would live as part of the buyer journey from now on, and we needed to get it right. We transformed the website within a month.

"It's time," I said to David.

"Finally," he said with excitement. This is what he had been waiting for.

We were ready to build ClearTrack's Go-To-Market.

4

GO-TO-MARKET STRATEGY

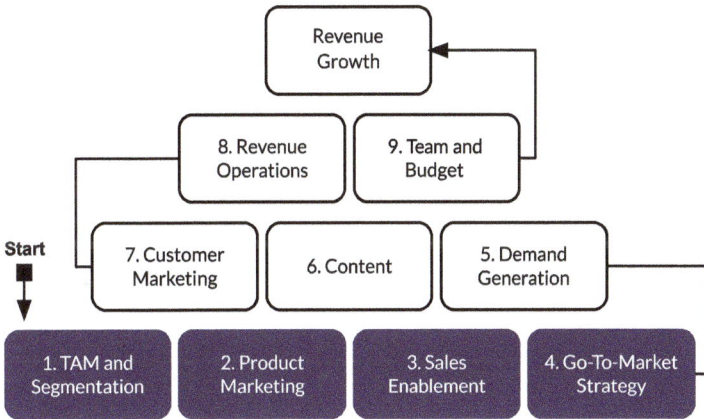

"What's the value of the largest customer you have?" I asked David.

"We've got three customers who are each paying over $100K per year," said David, "plus three customers each paying about $75K per year. Then we've got another nineteen customers paying $50K each."

Those twenty-five customers made up $1.625M of ClearTrack's ARR, which was about 23 percent of its overall $7,125,000 run rate.

ACV	Customers	Revenue	% of Revenue	NRR
$100,000+	3	$450,000	6.3%	130%
$75,000	3	$225,000	3.2%	125%
$50,000	19	$950,000	13.3%	110%
$25,000	73	$1,825,000	25.6%	105%
$10,000	203	$2,030,000	28.5%	95%
$5,000	329	$1,645,000	23.1%	50%

Meanwhile, more than 500 of ClearTrack's customers were smaller in size, averaging deal sizes of $10K or less, and made up 51.6 percent of revenue.

"Luckily, we don't have revenue concentration risk," said David, with pride. He knew that revenue concentration was one of the reasons why acquisitions fell apart.

"That's true," I responded. "Unfortunately, you have a different problem. The largest segment of your customers has the worst Net Revenue Retention."

ClearTrack's issue was that most of its customers were on the smaller end of the spectrum who also were not great fits for its solution. With such poor retention rates, ClearTrack was losing half of those customers every single year and needed to replace them to maintain its revenue levels.

"This had to be a big part of why Pinnacle held off on investing," I told David. "So much of your revenue is dependent on customers who are shrinking their business with you over time, which is just too much risk."

"We discussed this problem at length," admitted David, sounding defeated. "What can we do though? That's just the reality of our business."

"It's a reality because of how we currently Go-To-Market," I said.

CHOOSING THE RIGHT APPROACH

What kinds of customers a business reels in is a function of what channels and activities it invests in. As a general rule, the higher the price and Annual Contract Value (ACV) of a product, the lower the Total Addressable Market. As the ACV decreases, the TAM increases.

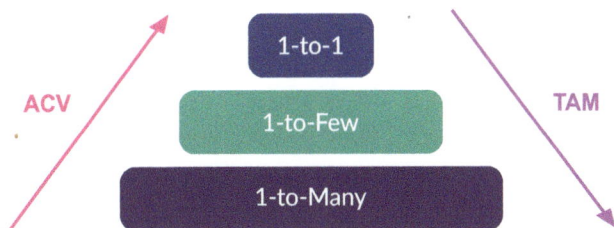

These two dimensions largely govern what avenues a particular business should take because as ACV shrinks, a company has a much lower amount of CAC to work with to have a healthy Payback Period. To put it another way: when deal sizes are smaller, you need to invest fewer dollars to acquire customers in order to break even in a reasonable amount of time.

When there is a mismatch between the approach a company should take and the one it actually takes, havoc ensues:

- The chosen channels are ineffective and conversion rates are significantly lower
- CAC gets inflated as companies spend too much to acquire customers
- Too many of the wrong fit customers come in the pipeline and end up churning too quickly

This is where ClearTrack went wrong. By not understanding its ideal-fit customers, the distribution of prospects it was bringing in was out of sync. In most months, the majority of deals ClearTrack was closing were in the $5K–10K range. Most of those customers were churning within the first year.

"Where are most of these demos coming from?" I asked Katie, trying to understand why we were bringing in so many of the wrong-fit customers.

Verticals and Segments	Avg. Demos per Month	Demo to Opp	Opp to Close	Avg. Deals Per Month	NRR
$75,000+	1	20%	30%	0	125%
$50,000	5	30%	35%	0–1	110%
$25,000	9	40%	40%	1–2	105%
$10,000	15	25%	30%	1–2	95%
$5,000	26	20%	30%	2–3	50%

"Most of our customers find us through the website," she replied. "It's through organic traffic and paid search."

I sat down with Katie to break down those traffic sources. Most of ClearTrack's traffic was coming from the following cluster of keywords in both Paid Search and SEO:

· Project Management Tools
· Project Management Software
· Kanban Software
· Scrum Software
· Project Management Checklist
· Project Management Templates

No wonder most of the customers coming through these sources were bad-fit customers. They were incredibly generic campaigns, targeted at anyone looking for Project Management software (more on this later). They were competing with behemoths like

Asana, Monday, and Trello for these keywords. On top of it all, none of them were connected to ClearTrack's best-fit verticals and customers.

"This is a recipe for disaster," I explained to David. "We need to invest our limited marketing dollars in targeting our ICPs."

In most companies, the best-fit customers usually make up more than one segment. ClearTrack was no different. Coming back to our market penetration data, ClearTrack had less than 1 percent of the market in its top verticals and less than 3 percent when looking at larger customers.

Vertical	Customers	Total Market	Customers (>10 seats)	Large Accounts (>10 seats)
Engineering	95	14,500	45	4,200
Architecture	67	7,500	39	1,200
Consulting	52	67,000	31	12,500
Legal	44	36,000	28	5,700
Accounting	29	25,000	17	3,100

What's more is that within the market of potential accounts with more than ten seats, there was a subset of target companies with more than 100 employees that represented much larger deal sizes. Most of those deals would have been more than $100K, and some more than $200K.

"How good of a fit is ClearTrack with those larger customers?" I asked David.

"We don't see a lot of them, but we're definitely competitive with the alternatives," he said. "A lot of them end up using Salesforce with a lot of customizations, which isn't a great fit for what they need."

ClearTrack had a few of these customers, which somewhat validated David's perspective. None of these customers were in the Legal or Accounting verticals, which made sense as those verticals had more tailored solutions. Within Engineering, Architecture, and Consulting alone, however, there were 300 targets that made up $128M in revenue potential.

Vertical	Customers	Customer $	Total Market	Revenue Potential
Engineering	1	$150,000	45	$29,000,000
Architecture	1	$125,000	75	$42,000,000
Consulting	1	$175,000	180	$57,000,000

Just looking at this data, it became clear that ClearTrack needed a different strategy for each of its segments. It needed to use a 1-to-Many approach for its smaller accounts; it needed to use a 1-to-Few approach for its mid-sized accounts, and it needed to use a 1-to-1 approach for its enterprise accounts.

Vertical	Seats	Total Market	Revenue Potential	GTM Approach
Small	<10	123,000	$450M	1-to-Many
Mid-Sized	10–99	26,700	$650M	1-to-Few
Enterprise	100+	300	$128M	1-to-1

Each segment's revenue was worth pursuing, assuming the right amount of effort. The Small accounts were worth it if they came purely inbound and self-serve, without eating too much CAC. The Mid-Sized were worth it with their larger deal sizes and high net retention rates, including investing more Marketing and Sales dollars. The large accounts were worth the customized effort because of the amount of revenue potential sitting in a few accounts.

"With the current marketing approach, most of the demos we're seeing each month are from the Small segment because there was no focus on landing the larger accounts," I explained to David. "That's what we're going to change."

INVESTING IN THE RIGHT CHANNELS

Depending on the segment you're going after, different channels are relevant.

A low ACV with a large TAM and many targets likely needs to focus on SEO, Paid Search, and Paid Social. Conversely, having a high ACV with a limited TAM and few targets implies the need for ABM, Sales Enablement, and Customer Marketing.

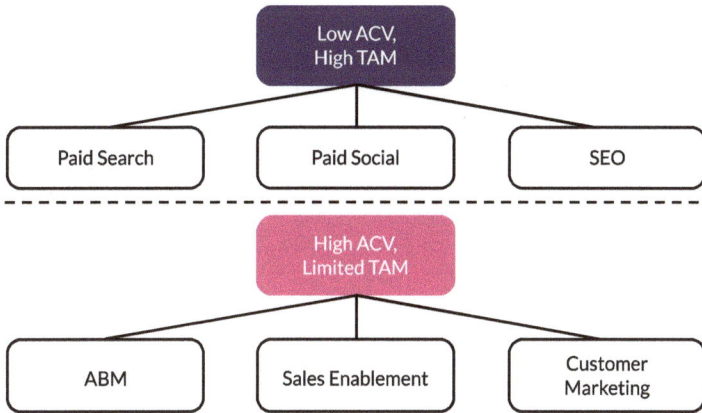

Knowing which channels, programs, and campaigns apply to which segments is critical to setting the right Go-To-Market strategy and allocating the right budget to those activities.

A quick way to think about this is as a matrix that's sorted by ACV. At each level, it is obvious which channels are more or less relevant than others.

"The problem is most of Katie's efforts have been focused on channels most relevant to smaller deal sizes," I explained to David, showing him the channel matrix. "This is a big part of the reason why Bryan and his team have complained about bad-fit leads in the pipeline."

ACV	Paid Media	SEO	ABM	Customer Marketing	Product Marketing	Corporate Marketing	Channel Partners	Sales Enablement
< $1K	Neutral	Great-fit	Not a good channel	Great-fit	Great-fit	Not a good channel	Not a good channel	Not a good channel
$1–10K	Great-fit	Great-fit	Not a good channel	Great-fit	Great-fit	Not a good channel	Not a good channel	Not a good channel
$10–50K	Great-fit	Great-fit	Great-fit	Great-fit	Neutral	Neutral	Neutral	Great-fit
$50–300K	Neutral	Neutral	Great-fit	Great-fit	Great-fit	Great-fit	Great-fit	Great-fit
$300K+	Neutral	Not a good channel	Great-fit	Great-fit	Great-fit	Great-fit	Great-fit	Great-fit

Not a good channel	Neutral	Great-fit channel

ClearTrack needed to build out a channel matrix for the different segments it had identified.

Vertical	GTM	Priority	Channels
Small	1-to-Many	Low	SEO, Paid Media, Referral
Mid-Sized	1-to-Few	High	Paid Media, SEO, ABM, Events, Customer Marketing
Enterprise	1-to-1	Medium	ABM, Events, Customer Marketing

"For the Small segment, we need to filter them into a self-serve track before they ever talk to Sales," I explained to Katie and Bryan. "We can't waste the Sales team's time on these leads."

Instead, the smaller accounts could go through a free trial and then upgrade to a paid account. On the programs' front, I asked Katie to turn off all generic Paid Media campaigns that were bringing in the smaller accounts (more on this later). Instead, the only way ClearTrack would land small accounts was through organic or referral sources. This basically meant the CAC was zero, so it was fine even if the customer churned in less than a year.

For the enterprise accounts, we needed a full list of named accounts for the three hundred targets. Then, we needed to select a handful of accounts to begin a collaborative account-based Marketing and Sales process. This required a lot of heavy lifting in the form of customized content and outreach.

For the mid-sized accounts, the focus needed to be on Paid Media, SEO, Events, and ABM. The ABM work wasn't going to be 1-to-1 like for the Enterprise segment, but instead more of a 1-to-Few approach. For Paid Media and SEO, ClearTrack needed to shift away from the generic programs Katie and her team had been running to focus on more directly relevant clusters of campaigns where the best fit verticals could be targeted with customized benefits and outreach.

"We need to eventually get to all of these activities," I said to David.

"It seems so obvious now. But how can we fund all of this work?" He asked.

David was right. Doing all this work at once was unrealistic. It was going to take months to go after a handful of enterprise accounts, and the ClearTrack team didn't have enough bandwidth to do that work along with everything else that needed to be done.

"This is why we need to prioritize where to start," I responded.

ALLOCATING THE RIGHT FOCUS

It's important to understand that this focus would be quite different for ClearTrack's different segments. Customizing the channel matrix for ClearTrack's segments looks like this:

Vertical	Paid Media	ABM	SEO	Events	Customer Marketing
Small	Medium	Low	High	Low	Low
Mid-Sized	High	High	Medium	Low	Medium
Enterprise	Medium	High	Low	Medium	High

The mid-sized accounts were where ClearTrack really needed to focus. That's where the bulk of the market and revenue opportunities were. There were enough targets to drive the volume ClearTrack needed to hit its goal of $3M in new ARR and $9M in pipeline, given that opportunities convert at 33 percent.

Starting with a 1-to-Few approach also gave ClearTrack exposure to down-market opportunities while reaching enterprise accounts.

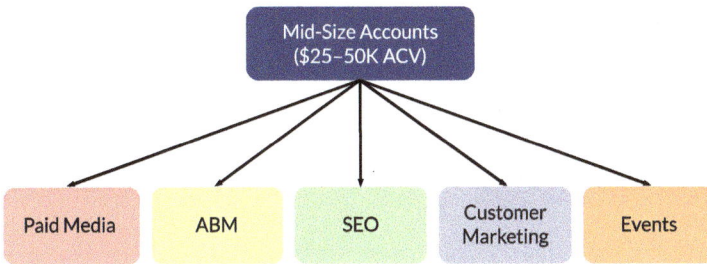

I worked with Katie to build a list of prioritized projects across these five channels. The key was to focus on the 1-to-Few approach to ensure that the smaller or bad-fit customers were not entering the pipeline.

Channel	Focus Level	Activities

Paid Media	High	• Focus on Paid Search, listing, and Paid Social campaigns related to top verticals
		• Examples:
		  ○ "Engineering firm software"
		  ○ "Architecture firm software"

ABM	High	• Build customized experiences for each vertical with targeted messaging, offers, content, and landing pages • Build email cadences and outbound sequences to enable the sales team • Target larger accounts via account-based Paid Media campaigns

SEO	Medium	• Build content focused on ranking for the most relevant terms for top verticals
		• Prioritize late funnel keywords—similar to Paid Media terms
		• Prioritize mid- and early funnel keywords that can be used to capture more volume in traffic and leads and nurture them to demo
		• Examples:
		  ○ "Tools for Engineering Firms"
		  ○ "Time tracking tools for Professional Services"

Customer Marketing	Medium	• Sell more seats to existing customers • Increase prices • Capture a percentage of payments volume as revenue
Events	Low	• Focus on industry-specific Trade Shows for top verticals, instead of more generic conferences • Limit the number to a handful per year (3–5) instead of trying to compete on Project Management at conferences all year round

"This is where we need to double down our focus on the best-fit customers and verticals," I said to Katie.

Another way to visualize the above focus is as a pie chart. The channels requiring the biggest focus should make up the bulk of your attention, activities, and budget. In ClearTrack's case, this meant that Paid Media and ABM had to make up most of its Marketing team's focus.

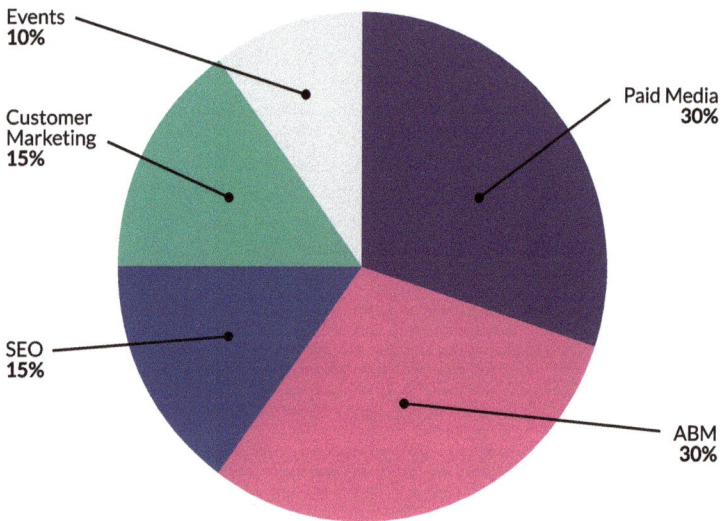

Events
10%

Paid Media
30%

Customer
Marketing
15%

SEO
15%

ABM
30%

When looking at where Katie and her team were previously focused, it was entirely different from the above. Most of their work was going into SEO and generic Paid Media campaigns, which were bringing in the wrong-fit leads, which led to Bryan and his team complaining, which led to lack of alignment, which led to poor retention rates.

This is the vicious cycle companies find themselves in when their Go-To-Market strategy doesn't have the right focus.

"I see now why we've been having so many problems," said David, realizing the underlying problems with ClearTrack's old approach.

"We've got to take this even further," I said. "Now that ClearTrack is focused in the right direction, we need to scale up our demand gen and content efforts to drive more pipeline."

5

DEMAND GENERATION

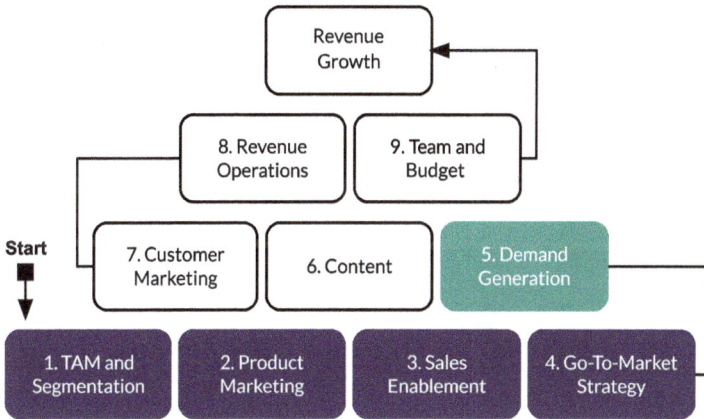

"I just don't have enough visibility," said David. "That's why it's been hard to hold Katie and the Marketing team accountable."

"How often are you tracking Marketing's impact on revenue?" I asked.

"We've never done that," he responded. "I have revenue targets for Bryan and his team, but not for Marketing."

"How are you holding Katie and her team accountable, then?" I pressed further.

"MQLs for the most part," David responded, sheepishly. He knew his answer wasn't great.

This was the problem. It's actually the same problem that plagues companies everywhere. Sales have revenue targets and quotas to hold them accountable. Meanwhile, Marketing has a Marketing Qualified Leads (MQLs) target. When Marketing brings in bad-fit leads, like Katie and her team had been doing at ClearTrack, Sales complains. The CEO then looks at dashboards to mediate the matter, and there is no way to figure out who is telling the truth.

Within the current operational structure, Marketing never had to measure which activity produces the most revenue. Because all MQLs are treated equally, the Marketing team's end goal is to simply fill the top of the funnel and report on that. After all, more MQLs mean you're doing a good job, right?

Not necessarily.

Every marketing activity produces a different kind of lead. Someone who downloads a whitepaper from a Paid Social ad and attends a webinar is completely different from someone who requests pricing. Marketing teams deploy lead scoring metrics in an attempt to evaluate lead quality. For example, if someone downloaded a whitepaper and then read three blog posts, they are converted to an MQL. This means Marketing is treating this lead as equal to someone who signed up for a product demo. The problem is these leads are anything but the same quality.

This is how bad MQLs enter the pipeline. Sales ends up complaining about lead quality, and MQL to Closed Won rates drop. Sales is pressured to try to make up for missing its quota. They're given new call scripts, objection handling responses, and competitive intelligence tools while being told they need to dial for dollars better. Meanwhile, if Marketing takes curtain calls at the weekly all-hands meeting about hitting an all-time high in MQLs generated, tension between the Marketing team and the sales reps erupts, which is why Sales teams end up hating Marketing in some organizations.

In ClearTrack's case, this lack of accountability led to Katie and her team bringing in bad-fit customers that were smaller in size and had poor retention metrics. The mismatch in who Marketing needed to target and who they were actually bringing in went unnoticed because the right accountability framework wasn't in place.

"This isn't Katie's fault," I said, being candid with David. "It's yours. You've got to hold Katie accountable to revenue. That's the only way she and Bryan will be able to move the ball forward together."

BUILDING THE RIGHT
ACCOUNTABILITY FRAMEWORK

David and I sat together with Katie and made it clear that Marketing's core accountability going forward was going to change.

"From this point forward, we will be reporting on two core metrics," I said. "Marketing Generated Pipeline and revenue."

By tracking beyond MQLs, we removed Marketing's bias for MQL volume. If Bryan and the Sales team had a qualification call with a prospect that they thought was a bad fit for any reason, then that lead was removed from the pipeline generated by Marketing. Simple.

"I feel like Bryan is just going to shift the blame back to us," said Katie.

"Sales wants to close more deals because their entire compensation structure depends on it," I insisted to Katie. "You need to trust Bryan and the Sales team because we all want the same outcomes. If they give us feedback on lead quality, we need to take that seriously."

Based on my deep dive with David and his team so far, I knew a few things. I knew that ClearTrack was bringing in a lot of bad-fit customers. I knew the Sales team was complaining about having demos with prospects who were too small. And I knew that Katie was investing in campaigns that were too generic.

By having the right accountability framework for Marketing, we now had an ongoing mechanism to measure its effectiveness so that the whole company was on the same page. Marketing stopped reporting on vanity metrics like lead volume and began focusing on pipeline and revenue. Every time Sales accepted the lead, they were signaling that the lead quality was good, and it could no longer be used as a reason for missing quota.

This allowed everyone to focus on high-quality prospects who were actually ready to enter the next stage of the funnel. It also removed channel bias. Given that some channels were generating leads who were more ready to buy than others, Marketing Generated Pipeline told us how many of those leads were actually accepted by Sales. At the MQL level, this is impossible to accomplish with just lead scoring mechanisms. Now that a sales rep had to call a prospect to verify lead quality, there was new clarity about which channels brought in the best leads.

Most importantly, this change removed excuses on both sides and completely upended the legacy dynamics inside ClearTrack. Instead, the company began ushering in a new era of alignment and teamwork between Marketing and Sales.

AUDITING EXISTING SPEND AND MAXIMIZING EFFICIENCY

"Now that we know what we are accountable for," I said to Katie, "we need to figure out how well we've been doing with our Marketing spend so far."

"How do we do that?" asked Katie.

"Let's start by looking at the amount of pipeline and revenue each of our channels is generating," I said.

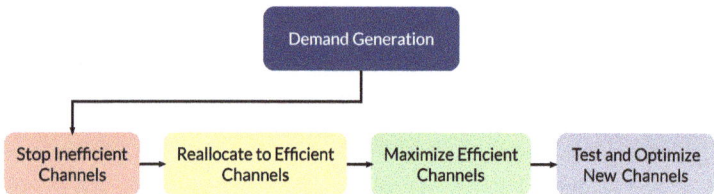

Because most companies don't look at the underlying data of their marketing spend, there is a lot of inefficiency to be found. This inefficiency means that a lot of budget is misallocated to channels and campaigns that are not very good at driving revenue. I've audited companies that can find 20–50 percent increased pipeline and revenue simply by auditing their existing spend and reallocating to more efficient channels. ClearTrack was no different.

I asked Katie to pull pipeline and Closed Won metrics for each channel she was investing in. I was very specific about which metrics I wanted to see:

- Spend ($)
- Marketing Qualified Leads (MQLs)
- Number of deals (SQLs)
- Marketing Generated Pipeline ($)
- Closed Won Revenue ($)
- Customer Acquisition Cost (CAC)
- Payback Period (Months)

"I'm not even sure if we have all these numbers," said Katie.

It was a response I had heard before. Most Marketing teams live inside Marketing systems without ever tying the data to Sales metrics. In Katie's case, all her metrics were inside HubSpot, while Bryan and his team were living inside Salesforce.

"It's okay," I said. "This doesn't need to be perfect. We need to get reporting that's good enough to make some good decisions."

It would have been tempting to enter a deep Revenue Operations cycle, overhaul systems, and take months to get the report we needed to get started. This is often where teams get stuck. Instead, doing things that don't scale is one of the fastest ways to get the insights required to scale. A duct-taped beta version that's available faster and allows you to triangulate the truth is better than a streamlined data warehouse that takes weeks or months to stand up. You can always increase reporting sophistication later. An iterative approach allows us to build pipeline faster.

I worked with Katie and her team to build a customized data spreadsheet. The attribution wasn't exact, but it gave us some concrete insights to make adjustments.

Channel	Spend	MQLs	Deals	Pipeline	Revenue	CAC	Payback Period
Paid Search	$80,000	13	1	$75,000	$25,000	$80,000	38 months
Trade Shows	$100,000	10	1	$70,000	$30,000	$100,000	40 months
Partners	$10,000	14	1	$90,000	$20,000	$10,000	6 months
Organic	$30,000	34	2	$225,000	$55,000	$15,000	7 months
Webinars	$25,000	22	2	$140,000	$60,000	$12,500	5 months
PR	$40,000	7	1	$30,000	$25,000	$40,000	19 months

Looking at these numbers, it became clear that Katie and her team were investing a lot of money on Paid Search, Trade Shows, and PR that was ineffective while not spending a whole lot of budget on partners and organic channels. Even though SEO was generating a lot of leads, they were not from the best-fit customers, and ClearTrack hadn't been investing strategically in scaling this channel.

"Does this mean we shouldn't invest in these channels?" asked David.

"Not exactly," I explained. "We need to drill down a layer deeper to understand what makes these channels ineffective in the first place."

When Marketing is managed at an executive dashboard level, a lot of insights are missed. The devil is in the details. Was it possible that ClearTrack shouldn't put any money into Trade Shows going forward? Sure it was. What was more likely was that ClearTrack was investing in the wrong programs within each of its inefficient channels.

This is where the Product Marketing work from Chapter 2 and the Go-To-Market approach from Chapter 4 really come together. The more aligned our actual programs are with our overall strategy, the more likely we are to be efficient with our overall Marketing spend. ClearTrack needed to connect its ICPs and best-fit customers to each channel and the programs within those channels.

This was the step that Katie had missed. Katie wasn't the only marketer making this mistake. Hundreds of millions of dollars are wasted annually by marketers on inefficient channels, campaigns, and programs. When companies are growing, these mistakes hide in plain sight. When companies falter, Marketing budgets are the first to get cut.

"In a world where data is so readily available," I explained to Katie, "there isn't any excuse for not having a more efficient Marketing effort."

I asked Katie to pull the same numbers above at a campaign and program level within the Paid Search, Trade Shows, and PR channels. Here is what we found:

Paid Search	Spend	MQLs	Deals	Pipeline	Revenue	CAC	Payback Period
Project Management	$30,000	3	0	$20,000	$0	n/a	n/a
Task Management	$20,000	1	0	$0	$0	n/a	n/a
Competitors	$11,000	2	0	$0	$0	n/a	n/a
Time Tracking	$8,000	3	1	$40,000	$25,000	$8,000	4 months
Professional Services	$6,000	2	0	$15,000	$0	$0	n/a
Resource Planning	$5,000	2	0	$0	$0	$0	n/a

Events	Spend	MQLs	Deals	Pipeline	Revenue	CAC	Payback Period
SaaS Events	$35,000	3	0	$25,000	$0	n/a	n/a
Project Management Events	$40,000	3	0	$20,000	$0	n/a	n/a
Professional Services Events	$25,000	4	1	$25,000	$30,000	$25,000	10 months

PR	Spend	MQLs	Deals	Pipeline	Revenue	CAC	Payback Period
SaaS Publications	$10,000	2	1	$25,000	$25,000	$10,000	5 months
Business Publications	$20,000	2	0	$5,000	$0	n/a	n/a
Professional Services Publications	$10,000	3	0	$0	$0	n/a	n/a

When summarized like this, the problem is easy to spot. Over 80 percent of ClearTrack's spend across all these channels was on generic campaigns focused on Project Management and bad-fit verticals. These channels had been bringing in a reasonable number of leads, but these weren't translating to deals and revenue. Katie was shocked to see the number of zeros when we broke down the impact like this.

Beyond this, ClearTrack actually had profitable campaigns sitting inside each channel. It just hadn't invested enough dollars into those channels because Katie and her team had not been revenue accountable until now. As expected, the most profitable campaigns were the ones that focused on the best-fit customers. Unfortunately, they received the least amount of spend.

"We need to flip our approach immediately," I said to Katie. "I want 80 percent of our spend going to our best-fit verticals."

I had Katie shut off all inefficient campaigns. Between the Paid Search, Trade Shows, and PR channels, this equated to around $200K in annual spend. The Payback Period on this spend was over thirty-two months on average.

Katie remarked, "I can't believe we've wasted so much of our budget on these campaigns."

I nodded. "This is why we do this work."

Tracking CAC and Payback Periods are critical pieces to keeping Marketing spend at healthy levels across channels and programs. Payback Period is helpful in particular as it adjusts for the size of deals coming in, not just volume. A higher CAC is acceptable for larger deals. By doing this exercise at a campaign level, we can see which channels bring in larger deals.

"The good news is we have $200K in Marketing budget to invest without going to the board," I said to Katie.

By focusing on the right accountability metrics and efficiency, we had found more spend to allocate to our more profitable efforts. The first step was to double down and maximize budget allocation to channels and campaigns where our best-fit customers were being found.

Channel	Historic Annual Spend	Historic Annual Revenue	Historic Payback Period	Adjusted Annual Spend	Adjusted Expected Revenue	Adjusted Payback Period
Paid Search	$80,000	$25,000	38 months	$50,000	$50,000	12 months
Trade Shows	$100,000	$30,000	40 months	$40,000	$30,000	16 months
Partners	$10,000	$20,000	6 months	$35,000	$40,000	11 months
Organic	$30,000	$55,000	7 months	$90,000	$95,000	11 months
Webinars	$25,000	$60,000	5 months	$60,000	$75,000	10 months
PR	$40,000	$25,000	19 months	$10,000	$15,000	8 months

Just by doing this exercise, we could forecast an increase in Marketing Generated Revenue of over 42 percent. Most of this increase sat inside Paid Search and organic as there were a ton of campaigns and keywords focused on ClearTrack's top verticals that Katie and her team had either overlooked or underinvested in.

This wasn't an abnormal increase, by the way. Every company we've ever audited has similar inefficiencies. By simply going through an exercise of reallocating spend away from inefficient activities to more efficient ones, we've seen companies increase Marketing Generated Pipeline and Revenue between 30-50 percent. It is sometimes shocking how much of the Marketing budget is being wasted when the right accountability framework and oversight isn't in place.

Now that David finally had the visibility he wanted, we needed to scale our Marketing spend wherever we could drive growth profitably. We looked through the potential to maximize spend in each channel where average Payback Periods stayed around twelve months.

Often, you can find additional opportunities by maximizing the return from existing activities. This is another exercise where companies can uncover 50–200 percent in additional Marketing Generated Pipeline without adding a net new channel, program, or activity. In ClearTrack's case, we found we could increase in spend on existing channels by 225 percent, while driving 200 percent more revenue from the same channels. Doing these two activities alone unlocked a new stratum of growth for ClearTrack.

Channel	Adjusted Annual Spend	Adjusted Expected Revenue	Adjusted Payback Period	Maximized Annual Spend	Maximized Expected Revenue	Maximized Payback Period
Paid Search	$50,000	$50,000	12 months	$115,000	$105,000	13 months
Trade Shows	$40,000	$30,000	16 months	$90,000	$80,000	14 months
Partners	$35,000	$40,000	11 months	$100,000	$105,000	11 months
Organic	$90,000	$95,000	11 months	$175,000	$165,000	13 months
Webinars	$60,000	$75,000	10 months	$130,000	$120,000	13 months
PR	$10,000	$15,000	8 months	$30,000	$35,000	10 months

"I always had a feeling we were spending money on the wrong activities," said David, shocked by how much inefficiency and opportunity we found.

"Now that we have this framework in place, we have a way to rebalance, reallocate, and maximize our marketing budget and efficiency on an ongoing basis," I responded.

TESTING NEW CHANNELS AND PROGRAMS

"This alone is a significant roadmap for us to work through," said Katie, feeling overwhelmed by the amount of work ahead for her small team.

"We're not done yet," I said. "We still haven't looked at additional avenues that connect to our overall Go-To-Market strategy."

The work we had done in Chapter 4 was now going to add additional focus areas for Katie's team. With efficiency in a good place, it was time to look at additional avenues for ClearTrack to scale its demand generation efforts.

As a refresher, this is where we decided that ClearTrack needed to focus to target its different segments.

Vertical	Paid Media	ABM	SEO	Events	Partners
Small	Medium	Low	High	Low	Low
Mid-Sized	High	High	Medium	Low	Low
Enterprise	Medium	High	Low	Medium	High

While our work so far had scaled up efforts related to Paid Media, we had yet to focus on ABM. It's natural for things to go this way. There is often so much opportunity in the channel reallocation and maximization exercises that companies sometimes don't get to new channels until much later. Companies get to this stage and find that their Paid Media efforts are unoptimized. This is where the Go-To-Market strategy build out we did in the last chapter is critical.

Coming back to our market penetration data, ClearTrack had less than 1 percent of the market in its top verticals and less than 3 percent when looking at larger customers.

Vertical	Customers	Total Market	Customers (>10 seats)	Large Accounts (>10 seats)
Engineering	95	14,500	45	4,200
Architecture	67	7,500	39	1,200
Consulting	52	67,000	31	12,500
Legal	44	36,000	28	5,700
Accounting	29	25,000	17	3,100

There was about $128M in value sitting within its largest segment of accounts within those same verticals.

Vertical	Customers	Customer $	Total Market	Revenue Potential
Engineering	1	$150,000	45	$29,000,000
Architecture	1	$125,000	75	$42,000,000
Consulting	1	$175,000	180	$57,000,000

"This is really where we need to focus," I told Katie pointing at the data on larger accounts.

With so much revenue inside the larger accounts of our best-fit verticals, prioritizing customized outreach to those accounts would allow ClearTrack to uncover significant growth.

I wanted Katie and her team to build for two tiers of ABM efforts:

1. 1-to-Few
    a. Build customized experiences for each vertical with targeted messaging, offers, content, and landing pages
    b. Build email cadences and outbound sequences to enable the Sales team
    c. Target larger accounts via account-based Paid Media campaigns

2. 1-to-1
   a. Identify ten to twenty named accounts, with asymmetrically large deal sizes, in each of our top verticals
   b. Build 1-to-1 campaigns in partnership with the Sales team to target larger accounts

Most companies largely misunderstand ABM. Jumping to 1-to-1 campaigns while there is so much opportunity on the 1-to-Few segments is one of the most common mistakes. By building out campaigns for tighter segments, companies often end up targeting their dream accounts from their named account list, anyway.

That being said, you still need to build customized campaigns for the highest value accounts. These tailored journeys can make the difference between closing or losing a seven-figure deal.

As a next step, we needed to determine how much focus to allocate to each type of campaign. I asked Katie to build out a list of accounts and segments and prioritize them by revenue potential, investment required, ROI, and Payback Period.

With such low penetration rates across its top verticals and enterprise customers, ClearTrack had the potential to land $3.2M in revenue in the next twelve months with CAC Payback Periods under 12 months for its top segments and customers.

Segments and Accounts	12-Month Revenue	Investment Required	ROI	Payback Period
Engineering ($50–75K)	$802K	$534K	1.50	8 months
Architecture ($50–75K)	$816K	$408K	2.00	6 months
Consulting ($50–75K)	$342K	$195K	1.75	7 months
Top 3 Engineering Accounts	$525K	$403K	1.30	9 months
Top 3 Architecture Accounts	$420K	$247K	1.70	7 months
Top 3 Consulting Accounts	$375K	$341K	1.10	11 months

This analysis is often skipped inside companies when it comes to larger segments and accounts. It's a lot easier to forecast and look at revenue potential for inbound volumes and Paid Media spend, for example, than it is to think about the revenue potential from landing larger customers. The reason for this is that landing larger accounts requires a broad set of activities that are not as easy to measure.

By analyzing how much revenue sits inside the larger segments and then forecasting out their propensity to buy and looking at the associated costs to capture that revenue, we can prioritize such campaigns against the spend of more obvious channels.

"I want just as much effort going into these accounts as we are currently spending on inbound," I said to David. "Katie and her team should allocate their focus accordingly."

Returning to our visualization of the pie chart from the last chapter, we can see an even greater reason for allocating our focus as we did.

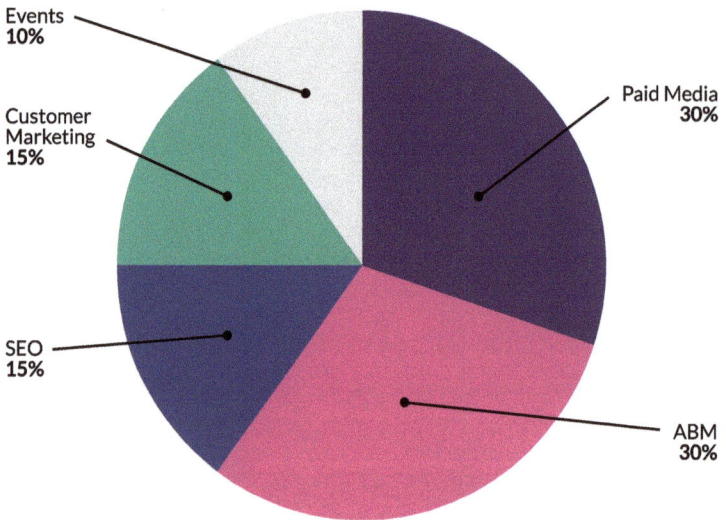

Events
10%

Customer
Marketing
15%

Paid Media
30%

SEO
15%

ABM
30%

This is how the Go-To-Market strategy we built comes to life. It influences key decisions on how we allocate our limited resources of people and budget.

"We are now ready to shift our focus to Content," I said to Katie. "We need to build the right roadmap to support all this work."

6

CONTENT

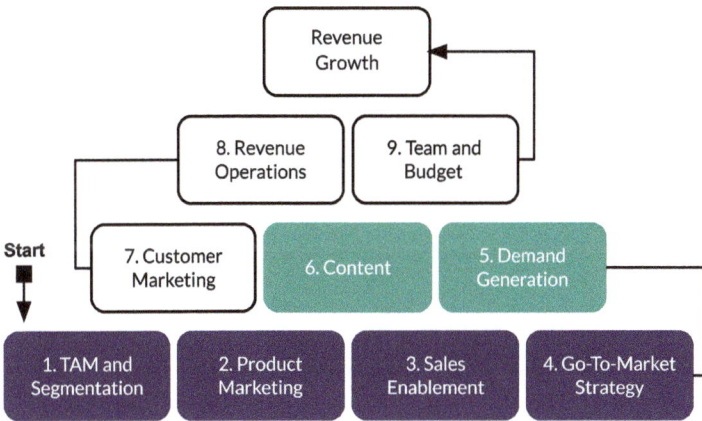

"Haven't we been working on content this whole time?" asked David.

It was a reasonable question. So far, we'd created:

- Product Marketing content on positioning and messaging

- Sales Enablement content so that reps could have better conversations
- Website content to help buyers self-serve their way through the buying process

"You're right. We have been," I responded. "Along the way, we've addressed some critical gaps in content. We still don't have a full content roadmap though."

While Demand Generation is *where* we invest our marketing efforts, content is *what* we show to customers. In ClearTrack's case, there were so many different priorities to consider in order to build a roadmap for content that would support the revenue goals. Plus, the legacy focus on categories like Project Management needed to change.

"We just do our best to keep up with requests," said Katie. "Outside of the SEO work we've done, we try to work through whatever the Sales and Product teams need from us."

Katie's Content team faced the same challenge that almost every Content team faces. Every function needs something from content because it has a major role to play at every stage of the customer journey. As a result, the Content team's work inevitably becomes reactive.

This was one of the reasons why ClearTrack's Go-To-Market had been so focused on generalized categories and verticals with lower conversion rates—the Content team just had too many items on its backlog to ever be more strategic.

Content is a lot like Product Management in this way. Product Management constantly faces requests from every part of the organization. Sales wants features that will help it overcome objections and close deals. Customer Success wants features that will help them onboard, expand, and retain accounts. Support wants bug fixes.

The list of what Product Management needs to sift through is endless. The only difference is that Product Management has an established process to sift through the noise in order to focus on its core objective of building a better solution for end customers.

Content, similarly, needs a process to sift through the noise. The challenge with Content is that it is extremely difficult to be intentional about what it wants to achieve. It is so easy to get distracted and pulled away from strategic initiatives because of the next fire that needs to be put out.

"We're going to shut out all content requests for the next quarter," I told David. "I need Katie and the team hyper-focused on creating the content we need to scale pipeline."

I walked David and Katie through the framework I wanted to use to prioritize our content efforts.

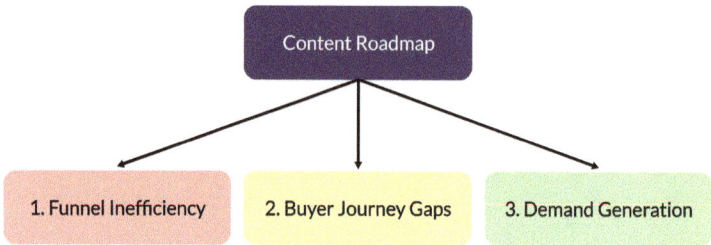

Once foundational content like Product Marketing, Sales Enablement, and website assets are in place, what's next is often difficult to figure out. This is where looking at the following is helpful to sort through the noise:

1. **Funnel Inefficiency:** Where are the biggest leaks in the funnel? How can content be leveraged to improve conversion rates?

2. **Buyer Journey Gaps:** Where are the biggest gaps in the buyer journey? What do we need to help buyers get to the next stage in the funnel?

3. **Demand Generation:** What content do we need to support our demand generation efforts? How much revenue is attached to these initiatives?

With ClearTrack's updated focus on its top verticals and best-fit customers, all three areas needed more content.

UNCOVERING FUNNEL INEFFICIENCY

Looking at where inefficiencies exist in the funnel is the fastest way to uncover how content can make the biggest impact. ClearTrack actually had really good conversion rates for its top verticals and larger accounts. Smaller accounts were where most of its inefficiency in the funnel was coming from.

Here are the conversion rates for all the verticals and segments. As you can see, most of the inefficiency does not come from its best-fit customers.

Verticals and Segments	Avg. Demos per Month	Demo to Opp	Opp to Close
Engineering	5	45%	55%
Architecture	7	40%	45%
Consulting	4	35%	40%
Legal	3	24%	33%
Accounting	2	21%	28%
Construction	3	15%	22%
SaaS	10	11%	15%
Micro (<5 seats)	22	22%	20%

Despite being the lowest converting verticals across the board, Micro, SaaS, and Construction leads made up nearly 65 percent of the volume Marketing was bringing in. As noted in previous chapters, this disparity stemmed from Marketing's focus on generic keywords and campaigns in both Paid Search and SEO.

ClearTrack did not need to necessarily improve how to convert its best-fit customers when they came in. It needed to meet more of its best-fit customers. With around 65 percent of its volume coming from bad-fit customers, the best form of funnel optimization was to improve the quality of traffic.

By not looking at their own funnel efficiency data, companies misunderstand where the biggest optimization opportunities actually are and also where content can make the biggest impact. Depending on the root cause of your Funnel Inefficiency, the antidote is different.

Problem Area	Action Steps
Website Traffic	Scale SEO content production and backlinking
Traffic to Demo Rate	Improve landing pages, web experience, and technical SEO
Demo to Opp	Create better nurture programs and experiences
Opp to Close	Enable the Sales team with better resources

If your Opportunity to Close rates are weak, you need to create more assets for the Sales team to help them close more deals. If your Demo to Opp rates are weak, odds are your nurture programs need to do a better job of converting prospects. If your Traffic to Demo rates are weak, landing pages and offers on those pages need improvement. And if your overall traffic is weak, you likely need to produce a lot more content to capture traffic from all sources.

In a lot of cases, the root cause is actually meeting the wrong customers. Companies like ClearTrack look at traffic and lead volumes being high and assume everything will just convert through the funnel. Fewer leads from the right audience is better than more leads from the wrong audience.

With the Product Marketing and website work we had done, ClearTrack had a lot of the right assets in place for its best-fit customers already. It just needed better traffic to drive to those pages.

For Paid Media, this meant shutting down all its generic campaigns. As noted in the last chapter, ClearTrack was spending over $200K annually on campaigns that had an average Payback Period of over thirty-six months. We then shut off that spend and directed it toward more profitable campaigns.

For SEO, the work here was a lot different than simply shutting off and reallocating spend. We didn't need ClearTrack to shut down any of its generic landing pages because they were a low-cost acquisition channel for smaller accounts, even if they were not the best fit.

Instead, we needed to build organic traffic in the right areas. This meant creating new content for the best-fit customers across the top, middle, and bottom of the funnel.

Clusters	Examples	Monthly Traffic
Top of Funnel	• How to optimize operations for Consulting firms • How to scale Engineering firms	110K
Middle of Funnel	• Workforce management for Engineering firms • Resource Planning for Architecture Firms	40K
Bottom of Funnel	• Engineering firm software • Architecture firm software • Consulting firm software • Time tracking software	15K

ClearTrack had previously never created content like this. While the above analysis is an extremely simplified version of all the identified opportunities, this approach opened up the possibility of scaling ClearTrack's monthly traffic by over 165,000 potential visitors. To capture this traffic, ClearTrack needed to invest in a roadmap of twenty-five core assets that could rank for all the terms involved.

"That's a lot of content to produce," said Katie. "Which ones should we start with?"

"Before we answer that," I said, "we have to identify all the other assets we need."

IDENTIFYING BUYER JOURNEY GAPS

With our focus on Funnel Inefficiency, we had identified additional assets required to drive better quality prospects into the funnel. What we haven't done is identify which assets are required to nurture those prospects through the funnel.

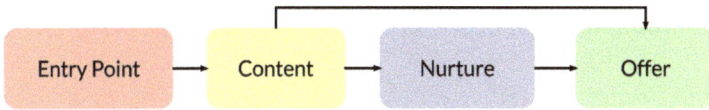

In most companies, there is often only one main path through the funnel. A prospect comes in through any entry point, fills out a form, is engaged by sales until the deal closes, or the prospect enters the Closed Lost column. ClearTrack was no different. The problem with this approach is that there is no nuance for where the prospect is on their journey, nor is there any consideration for who the prospect is and what makes them different.

This is where the entry point is actually the critical juncture where all marketing work intersects. Entry points are heavily dependent on persona, ICPs, vertical, industry, size, stage, and much more. You can cluster certain entry points together, but you cannot build uniform journeys for all.

ClearTrack was making this exact mistake. Its ICPs of Engineering, Architecture, and Consulting firms were being bunched up with anyone looking for Project Management software. We needed to change this.

At full maturity, entry points and the subsequent journeys cascade. Thousands of prospects move through thousands of independent journeys, all seemingly similar yet distinct in their messaging, positioning, content, and offers.

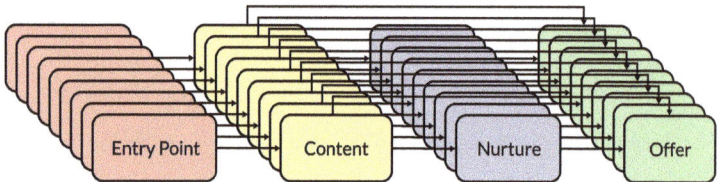

None of this is to say that the journeys don't or can't intersect. Someone in one journey may attend the same webinar as someone in another journey, for example. The key point to keep in mind is that companies need to build enough customization into their funnels to speak to their best-fit customers.

For ClearTrack, this meant building enough assets to support all the different entry points for our best-fit customers and verticals.

Notice how all the Product Marketing, website, and Sales Enablement work we did in earlier stages drastically reduced the number of assets ClearTrack needed to create. In most companies I encounter, the list is a lot longer because the foundational work has never been done (also worth noting that this list is simplified for the purposes of this book).

Segment	Assets Needed
Engineering	• "ClearTrack versus Engineering" Competitor pages • "Engineering firm software" consumer guide • Article on "best Engineering firm software" • Case study of client Engineering firm • Webinar on how to scale operations for Engineering firms • Benchmarking report for Engineering firms
Architecture	• "ClearTrack versus Architecture" Competitor pages • "Architecture firm software" consumer guide • Article on "best Architecture firm software" • Case study of client Architecture firm • Webinar on how to scale operations for Architecture firms • Benchmarking report for Architecture firms
Consulting	• "ClearTrack versus Consulting" Competitor pages • "Consulting firm software" consumer guide • Article on "best Consulting firm software" • Case study of client Consulting firm • Webinar on how to scale operations for Consulting firms • Benchmarking report for Consulting firms

The harsh truth is that there is absolutely no way to build an effective marketing engine for a company without building assets like this. Skipping this work is like not flossing. It will catch up to you.

UNDERSTANDING DEMAND GENERATION NEEDS

The last pillar to sort out was to identify all the assets our demand generation plans needed to scale pipeline. So far, we had already done a lot of the work required. Using our ICPs, best-fit verticals, and segments, we had:

· Updated the website with all key pages

- Reflected the updated messaging and positioning in all copy and content
- Optimized existing spend to focus on the most profitable campaigns
- Uncovered key SEO content required to drive better prospects to improve conversion rates throughout the funnel
- Identified core assets required across the buyer journey to nurture prospects more effectively

"Wow," said Katie. "We have made a lot of progress."

"When we do things in the right order, supporting demand generation doesn't look that complicated, does it?" I asked rhetorically.

There were only two areas left to address: Paid Media and ABM.

For Paid Media, we needed content to better engage our best-fit customers in all the channels we were investing in. For ABM, we needed more customized versions of the content we had created for our top segments.

On the Paid Media side, the work for Katie and her team was straightforward enough. It was similar to the work that they had done in the past.

On the ABM side, it required ClearTrack to develop a new kind of muscle. Landing enterprise accounts is a very different ball game and required a great deal of care and customization. To succeed, Katie needed to get far more involved with the Sales team.

Demand Gen Area	Assets Needed
Paid Media	• Update ads and copy across all channels • Build new entry points for each segment and vertical based on updated content assets • Produce new creative and offers for updated ICPs
ABM	• Build 1-to-1 Sales Enablement assets to engage top three accounts across Engineering, Architecture, and Consulting • Build 1-to-1 nurture assets for the top three accounts, such as ROI analysis • Build a multi-touch, multi-channel cadence for all key decision-makers at the top three accounts • Gather references for the top three accounts (secure customer evangelists in corresponding verticals) • Build customized pricing plans in partnership with Sales, Product, and the board

"I feel overwhelmed," said Katie. "This feels like way too much to manage."

"It is more than your current team can handle," I responded. "That's why we need to merge all this into a prioritized roadmap."

BUILDING A PRIORITIZED CONTENT ROADMAP

A framework I shared in my last book, *Post-Acquisition Marketing*, is the concept of laying Intent and Interest Stages across the buyer's journey to understand the needs of customers at every stage.

INTENT		
Awareness	**Knowledge**	**Consideration**

INTEREST	Awareness	Knowledge	Consideration
Hot	Needs expertise	Needs to know how software can solve a problem	Needs to test drive the software
Warm	Needs framework	Needs to understand the problem	Needs to evaluate software options
Cold	Needs to answer a question	Needs to answer a question	Needs software to solve a problem

Most companies don't fill out these quadrants for their prospective customers, nor do they start with the right content. The correct order of operations is to start on the top right and work your way backward to the bottom left.

INTENT		
Awareness	**Knowledge**	**Consideration**

INTEREST	Awareness	Knowledge	Consideration
Hot			
Warm		Work Backward!	
Cold			

In ClearTrack's case, all the work we had done to this point was about identifying the complete set of items that needed to be produced. We now just needed to prioritize it.

"Starting with people who are most ready to buy is always the right decision," I said to Katie. "It means making some hard choices, but they have to be made."

A more simplified way of looking at the above is to think about it in this way.

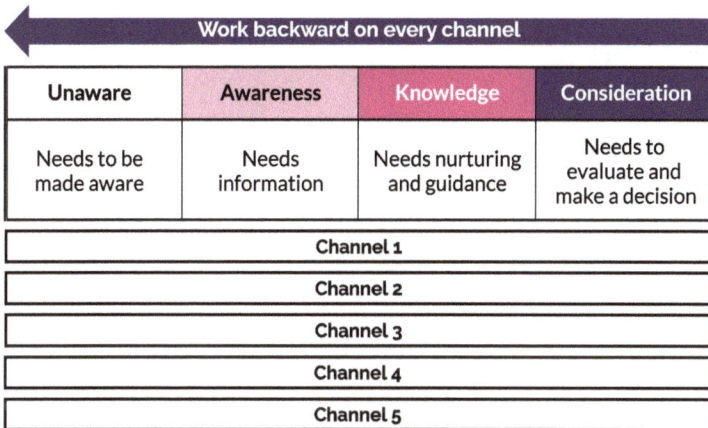

Work backward on every channel			
Unaware	**Awareness**	**Knowledge**	**Consideration**
Needs to be made aware	Needs information	Needs nurturing and guidance	Needs to evaluate and make a decision
Channel 1			
Channel 2			
Channel 3			
Channel 4			
Channel 5			

When you have so many competing priorities, simplify. Here is everything we had identified for ClearTrack:

Type	Awareness	Knowledge	Consideration
SEO	13 Assets	5 Assets	7 Assets
Nurture		8 Assets	10 Assets
Paid Media	11 Assets	7 Assets	5 Assets
ABM		5 Assets	9 Assets
Total	**24 Assets**	**25 Assets**	**31 Assets**

Doing this exercise made things very apparent. Katie and her team could not produce any other content until the thirty-one assets in the Consideration stage were completed.

"How long do you think it will take you to get through all this content production?" I asked Katie.

"About a quarter with everything else that's already in flight," she responded.

"Okay, that's reasonable," I said.

"Is it?" asked David. "I feel like a quarter is too long for us to wait on revenue impact."

"You can't rush these things," I pushed back, explaining why. "We've kept our roadmap to the bare essentials needed to scale. Moving faster than this would mean sacrificing something critical."

One of the reasons why companies never end up building all the right assets is because they never give themselves enough time to get it right the first time. The thing founders miss is that one way or another this work has to get done and the time has to be invested.

In companies that rush, the time is invested in the form of quick hiring and firing cycles for CMOs, missing revenue projections, and restarting initiatives that weren't taken to completion because short-term thinking was prioritized. In companies that get it right the first time, the front loaded effort of a quarter can save a lot of heartache and resources. It's one of those situations where the longer route is actually the shortest route.

Luckily, David bought into this journey. Companies need CEOs like David to be fully bought in to make their way through this transformation. It's the only way to make the right amount of progress.

"We've got one more critical area of programs to address," I said to David.

"What's that?" he asked.

"We need to make sure Marketing is doing everything in its power to maximize total customer value."

7

CUSTOMER MARKETING

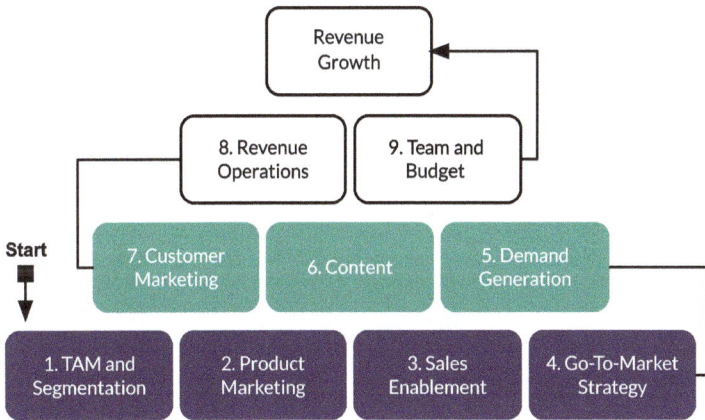

"This is something I've wanted to figure out for a long time," said David. "I'm guessing we have a lot of untapped revenue sitting inside our existing customers."

David, like many CEOs, had a tight connection to his customers and market. He knew there was more revenue to be captured within those accounts.

"How much effort is currently going into expanding existing accounts?" I asked.

"Almost none," he responded. "Most of our expansion revenue is ad hoc. We don't have a dedicated effort in this area."

This was not shocking to hear. Most companies focus all their growth efforts on landing new bookings. Expanding existing accounts is often a secondary objective. This is where companies and founders leave a lot of money on the table. To our point on the enterprise value of each additional dollar of revenue, prioritizing Customer Marketing can generate thousands, if not millions, more upon exit.

The more a company invests in expanding its Total Customer Value, the higher the likelihood of exit as well. A good way to think about it is to ask yourself, "What are some of the first things a buyer of this business would do upon acquisition to maximize their return?" While some would argue that leaving opportunities for the buyer to capture value from their investment is helpful, it's simply a lot better to have already captured this value because the asset overall is just more attractive to purchase. Again, it's better to sell a renovated home than a fixer-upper.

There are three core levers to maximize the Total Customer Value of existing customers:

1. **Seat Expansion:** Selling more users and growing current accounts
2. **Pricing:** Increasing how much customers pay for existing products and services
3. **Upsell/Cross-Sell:** Selling additional products and services

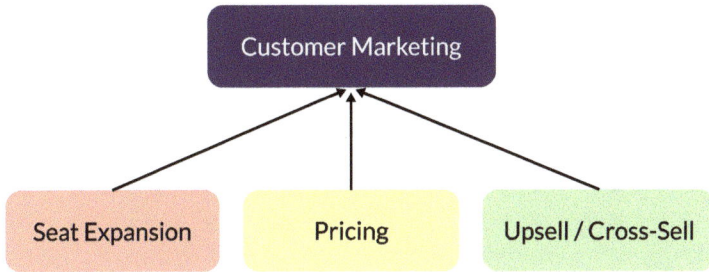

"We need to become more intentional about maximizing existing customer value," I said to David. "We need a plan of action for all three areas."

(Note: The sections in this chapter simplify strategies that involve much more detail. While the topics that follow could be separate books on their own, I felt it was necessary to include this chapter because Customer Marketing programs are critical to building a business to full maturity and must be factored into value creation plans. Also worth noting, we've excluded retention, as it is beyond the scope of this book.)

SELLING MORE SEATS

Coming back to our TAM and Segmentation data from the first chapter, it is amazing that ClearTrack's Net Revenue Retention was above 100 percent for its top verticals without a concerted effort being made in the area.

Vertical	Net Revenue Retention
Engineering	120%
Architecture	110%
Consulting	105%
Legal	95%
Accounting	92%
Construction	85%
SaaS	75%
Micro (<5 seats)	50%

What's more is that adjacent verticals like Legal and Accounting were right on the cusp of having a Net Revenue Retention rate of over 100 percent.

I worked with Bryan and Katie to analyze how many potential seats were out there within existing customers. We looked at current customers across the best-fit verticals and then looked at how many total open seats were inside those accounts. This gave us a focused universe to expand existing customer accounts.

Vertical	Customers	Customers (>10 seats)	Additional Potential Seats	Potential Revenue
Engineering	95	45	527	$316K
Architecture	67	39	441	$264K
Consulting	52	31	395	$237K
Legal	44	28	280	$156K
Accounting	29	17	207	$124K

Customers with smaller plans didn't have that many open seats because their entire teams had already adopted the solution. But customers with more than ten seats had a wider distribution of adoption. A lot of these customers had over ten seats, and some over a hundred seats.

Inside its existing base of customers, ClearTrack had the potential to capture $1.1M in additional revenue across its top five verticals, and $817K within its top three verticals. This amount represented a 17 percent increase in ClearTrack's current revenue run rate of $7M in ARR.

Even within the less-than-ideal verticals of Legal and Accounting with net retention rates of less than 100 percent, expanding the existing customers was worthwhile given their lower acquisition cost and Lifetime Value because the likelihood of expanding existing customers is a lot higher than landing new ones.

This is why Customer Marketing is so critical to the overall strategy. Coming back to our framework of working backward, the most productive and efficient type of revenue is revenue from existing customers because the CAC is as close to zero as you can get. The additional revenue is gravy on top that increases gross margins and Total Customer Value.

INCREASING PRICES

"Have you thought about increasing your prices?" I asked David.

"We haven't increased our prices since I started the company," said David. "I don't want to overcharge our customers and lose out to competitors."

David was voicing a fear I had heard from founders many times. They're afraid to raise prices because they don't want to break what's working. There's some logic to that. The origin of this logic, however, comes from focusing on the wrong types of customers.

Coming back to the Net Revenue Retention data, ClearTrack's top verticals were growing over time, not shrinking. Most of its net churn was coming from its smaller accounts and bad-fit verticals.

Vertical	Net Revenue Retention
Engineering	120%
Architecture	110%
Consulting	105%
Legal	95%
Accounting	92%
Construction	85%
SaaS	75%
Micro (<5 seats)	50%

"Increasing prices will only weed out your worst-fit customers," I said to David.

Looking at ClearTrack's customers by revenue only validated this logic. The net retention rates were north of 95 percent for all customers with an ACV of more than $10,000.

ACV	Customers	Revenue	% of Revenue	NRR
$100,000+	3	$450,000	6.3%	130%
$75,000	3	$225,000	3.2%	125%
$50,000	19	$950,000	13.3%	110%
$25,000	73	$1,825,000	25.6%	105%
$10,000	203	$2,030,000	28.5%	95%
$5,000	329	$1,645,000	23.1%	50%

When customers have net retention rates higher than 100 percent, they are telling you that your product is mission critical to what they do. That doesn't mean you should take advantage of the situation. It means you can and should set fair prices.

Given that ClearTrack had never increased its prices, the value per dollar invested by customers was increasing every year as David and his team improved the product, released more features, and added more capabilities. We needed to capture a lot of that lost value.

"One of the first things a PE firm will do once you're acquired is increase your prices," I said to David. "We may as well do that now to increase our expansion revenue and prove our stickiness."

With David's agreement, we modeled out the potential impact of increasing prices by 25 percent. We assumed an additional churn of 2 percent for the top segments, 5 percent for mid-tier accounts, and 20 percent for the smallest accounts.

ACV	Revenue	Revenue from 25% Increase	Additional Churn ($)	Net Impact
$100,000+	$450,000	$112,500	$9,000	$103,500
$75,000	$225,000	$56,250	$4,500	$51,750
$50,000	$950,000	$237,500	$19,000	$218,500
$25,000	$1,825,000	$456,250	$36,500	$419,750
$10,000	$2,030,000	$507,500	$101,500	$406,000
$5,000	$1,645,000	$411,250	$329,000	$82,250

David was shocked. "I can't believe we've been leaving so much money on the table." The net impact of the changes would total to $1.28M in added customer value.

By doing this work now, David had drastically increased his expansion revenue and increased his exit valuation. The best part about the exercise was that it increased ClearTrack's focus on its best-fit verticals by churning out customers who were obviously not a good fit. Now that ClearTrack knew who it was going after, losing the wrong people wasn't as painful.

EXPANDING THROUGH UPSELL AND CROSS-SELL

Coming back to the work we did in the Product Marketing chapter, ClearTrack shifting its focus to its best-fit customers meant shifting its product as well.

	Old	New
Ideal Customers	Any company needing Project Management software	Professional Services firms (Engineering, Architecture, Consulting, Legal, and Accounting)
Problem	Managing any project, large or small	Building the underlying framework for managing complex Professional Services engagements
Relevant Features	• Project and Task Management • Kanban Boards • Project Templates • Status Updates	• Project and Task Management • Time Tracking • Resource Planning • Budgeting and Forecasting
Competitors	Trello, Asana, Monday, Jira	BigTime, Kantata

As ClearTrack made this shift, features related specifically to its best-fit verticals became far more important. In particular, time tracking and invoicing became a workflow that ClearTrack's Product team identified as a critical feature to make the platform more critical for customers.

Usually, Upsell and Cross-Sell opportunities exist in companies with multiple products or modules. ClearTrack was a one-product company. The invoicing features, however, revealed a path to an additional revenue stream: payments.

Across its best-fit verticals, ClearTrack processed over $300M in annual payments. As it stood, this volume was not being monetized.

Vertical	Payments Volume	Revenue at 50 BPS
Engineering	$96M	$480,000
Architecture	$72M	$360,000
Consulting	$59M	$295,000
Legal	$44M	$220,000
Accounting	$37M	$185,000

If ClearTrack captured fifty basis points of this payment-processing volume, there was an additional $1.54M in revenue to capture from existing customers. To make this possible, ClearTrack's Product team needed to develop its invoicing and payments capabilities.

"We need to get the Product team to prioritize this work," I said to David. "We won't capture this revenue right away, but making progress here will help us tell a better story on the revenue upside."

David was excited. This was revenue he had not at all considered. He had his Product team hyper-focus on improving ClearTrack's invoicing and payments capabilities over the next two quarters. In the meantime, Katie and I started laying plans to run campaigns to increase payments adoption to capture this revenue.

"I feel guilty," confided Katie. "With so much critical work to do, I wish we could move faster."

"This is actually not a speed problem," I reassured her. "This is more of a resource problem."

Resourcing is the one big lever companies don't pull enough to get marketing ramped up faster. The reason? Marketers don't bring enough data to the table to justify additional spend. We were about to change that for Katie and ClearTrack.

"We're going to get you more help to move faster," I said to Katie. "But before we do, I want us to get all of our reporting and data in order."

8

REVENUE OPERATIONS

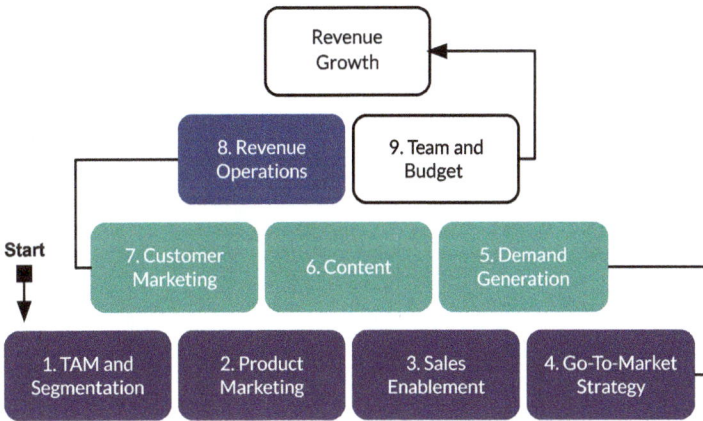

"I thought we already connected Marketing's work to revenue," said Katie. "What's missing?"

While we had already started the process for building a better data and reporting framework in Chapter 5 when we were analyzing ClearTrack's demand generation spend, we now needed to take that work to completion to get a full view of Marketing's performance and impact.

"What's missing is that we need to close the loop between Marketing's work and our overall business metrics," I responded. "That's how we get more resources."

What ClearTrack had so far was channel- and campaign-level reporting, which allowed it to measure spend versus performance for each channel. What it didn't have was a full Revenue Operations framework to run the marketing organization.

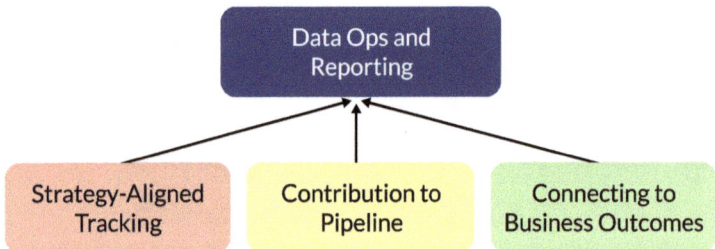

ClearTrack needed to measure:

1. **Metrics that aligned with strategy**: in order to measure progress for all activities that we had identified as focus areas.

2. **Overall Contribution to Pipeline**: in order to understand how much revenue Marketing was actually bringing in.

3. **Impact on Business Outcomes:** in order to see how Marketing's efforts were helping the business achieve its overall objectives.

Inside most companies, none of these reports exist or are being looked at regularly enough. ClearTrack was no different.

"With the work we've done to establish the right strategy, demand generation, and content roadmaps," I told Katie, "we now need to track those activities with the right dashboards to show progress."

Katie nodded. She understood that ClearTrack needed these metrics to become a more professionalized business.

"Showing progress with the right metrics," I continued explaining, "is how we get more budget and resources for Marketing."

ALIGNING TRACKING WITH STRATEGY

One of the big missed opportunities inside companies is they don't have an accurate data model built for their marketing engine. The key to building the right data model is to connect it to the chosen strategic path for the business. By doing so, companies can have a much better idea of which avenues are delivering more revenue than others.

Coming back to the pie chart from Chapter 4, ClearTrack's strategic focus was on Paid Media, ABM, SEO, and Events.

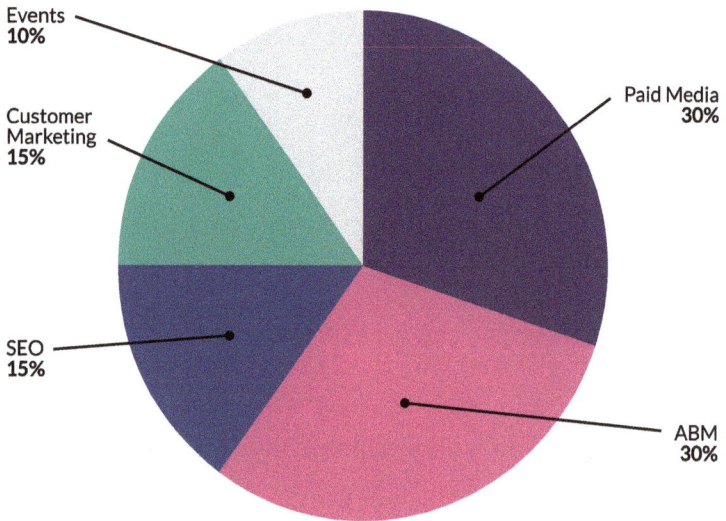

Events
10%

Customer
Marketing
15%

SEO
15%

Paid Media
30%

ABM
30%

"We need a full funnel dashboard for each channel," I instructed Katie. "And then we need all those metrics to merge into a combined dashboard."

I spent the next couple of weeks with Katie and her team building out basic dashboards for each strategic area.

Channel	Dashboard
Paid Media	• Overall Metrics ○ Total Spend ○ Impressions ○ Clicks ○ Visitors ○ Conversions ○ MQLs ○ SQLs ○ Closed Won Deals ○ Closed Won $ ○ CAC ○ Payback Period • Channel and Campaign Metrics ○ Paid Search ○ Paid Social ○ Listings and Directories ○ Display
SEO	• Overall Metrics ○ Domain Authority ○ Backlinks ○ High-Value Backlinks • Organic Metrics ○ Current Rank ○ Impressions ○ Clicks ○ Visitors ○ Conversions ○ MQLs ○ SQLs ○ Closed Won Deals ○ Closed Won $ • Keywork Metrics
ABM	• Overall Metrics ○ Spend ○ MQLs by Account and Vertical ○ SQLs ○ Closed Won Deals ○ Closed Won $ ○ CAC ○ Payback Period • Campaign Metrics ○ Target Accounts and Verticals ○ Contact Coverage ○ Account- and Vertical-Level Engagement ○ Pipeline from Top Accounts and Verticals versus Overall

Channel	Dashboard
Customer Marketing	• Seat Expansion # and $ from Existing Customers • Expansion Revenue $ from Pricing Increase • Payments Volume and Payments Revenue $

Events	• Overall Metrics
	  ○ Spend
	  ○ Captured Leads
	  ○ MQLs
	  ○ SQLs
	  ○ Closed Won Deals
	  ○ Closed Won $
	  ○ CAC
	  ○ Payback Period
	• Event-Level Metrics
	  ○ Spend
	  ○ Captured Leads
	  ○ MQLs
	  ○ SQLs
	  ○ Closed Won Deals
	  ○ Closed Won $
	  ○ CAC
	  ○ Payback Period

We had also identified different segments of customers that ClearTrack needed to go after.

Segment	GTM	Priority	Channels
Small	1-to-Many	Low	SEO, Paid Media, Referral
Mid-Sized	1-to-Few	High	Paid Media, SEO, ABM, Events, Customer Marketing
Enterprise	1-to-1	Medium	ABM, Events, Customer Marketing

This meant that not only did we need full funnel tracking by channel but also by customer type. These additional filters are often overlooked inside companies. For each of the above metrics, I had Katie segment out full funnel metrics by size and segment of customer, vertical, and geography to figure out where larger customers were coming from.

When combined, here is what Katie's top-level dashboard looked like for the past year, segmented by customer size.

Segment	Spend	MQLs	Pipeline	Deals	Revenue	CAC	Payback Period
Small	$358,000	267	$950,000	23	$276,000	$15,565	8 months
Mid-Sized	$250,000	245	$1,600,000	20	$500,000	$12,500	6 months
Enterprise	$200,000	160	$1,650,000	12	$504,000	$16,667	6 months

Then, each segment had a dashboard for each corresponding channel and activity so we could see where the revenue for each segment was coming from. For ABM programs, we needed an additional filter to track our top target accounts at each stage of the funnel. For Customer Marketing, we needed to track existing customers and how much pipeline and revenue is coming from different expansion avenues. All the dashboards were some variation of the above.

"This is a lot of data to sift through," said Katie.

"Yes it is," I responded. "But once we set this all up, it will provide an evergreen foundation from which we build all activities."

CALCULATING CONTRIBUTION
TO PIPELINE

With full funnel tracking in place, we were now ready to measure the overall impact Marketing was making on revenue.

"Don't we need to set up multi-touch attribution to do this right?" asked David. "I feel like we should invest in a technology solution that does this for us."

David was asking a reasonable question. It's a question companies ponder every year—should they invest in a Marketing attribution software to get their data tracking right?

"My answer to this is an unpopular take," I said to David. "This doesn't have to be that complicated. We need to get to a good enough state with tracking Marketing performance so we can make good decisions on where to allocate budget and how to scale."

Companies spend hundreds of thousands of dollars a year on getting attribution right. They debate over first-touch, last-touch, multi-touch, weighted models, and much more, while wasting precious time and money that can be allocated to something far more important: revenue growth.

A much better approach is to get metrics tracking to a place where you have enough insights to triangulate the truth so you can make better decisions. Then, you can move quickly to activities like demand generation programs, content creation, and Customer Marketing to move the needle on revenue.

ClearTrack needed to look at three overall metrics to figure out Marketing's overall impact:

1. **Marketing-Influenced Pipeline and Revenue:** how many deals and how much revenue did Marketing play a role in bringing in, nurturing, and converting?

2. **Marketing-Sourced Pipeline and Revenue:** how many deals and how much revenue did Marketing originally source?

3. **Percentage of Overall Pipeline and Revenue:** how much of the overall pipeline and revenue did Marketing actually source and influence?

Between these three metrics, sourced revenue is far more important because it tells us how much net new Revenue Marketing truly brought in. With this in mind, I had Katie pull up the following dashboard.

	MQLs	Pipeline	Deals	Revenue	CAC	Payback Period
Marketing Influenced	205	$1,400,000	20	$600,000	$14,250	6 months
Marketing Influenced %	30.5%	33.3%	36.4%	43.3%	n/a	n/a
Marketing Generated	100	$630,000	8	$215,000	$35,625	16 months
Marketing Generated %	14.9%	15.0%	14.5%	15.5%	n/a	n/a

As expected, Marketing Generated Revenue was significantly lower than Marketing Influenced. The Marketing Generated numbers represented all the different channels and activity metrics combined into overall numbers. The Influenced revenue, however, represented a much looser definition of Marketing impact, as it counted revenue from all other sources that Marketing barely touched.

"From now on, I want us to be accountable for Marketing Generated Pipeline only," I said to Katie.

"But we touch and help so many other leads," responded Katie. "How will we measure the impact of that?"

"We can still keep track of it," I said. "But we need to generate net new deals and revenue for the business if we want any chance of hitting our projections."

Too many Marketing leaders hide behind the Influenced pipeline to avoid accountability. If Sales sources and closes a deal but the contacts from that deal read a couple of blog posts, it is hardly a credit to the Marketing function that the deal closed. Minimum requirement interactions and engagements do not create more revenue. Instead, the Influenced pipeline tries to split the credit for a finite pie of revenue between more parties.

I had Katie take things a little further. I asked her to report on sourced pipeline based on the top verticals we identified.

	MQLs	Pipeline	Deals	Revenue	CAC	Payback Period
Marketing Generated Total	100	$630,000	8	$215,000	$35,625	16 months
Marketing Generated Engineering	9	$100,000	2	$50,000	$10,000	5 months
Marketing Generated Architecture	12	$140,000	2	$50,000	$9,000	4 months
Marketing Generated Consulting	7	$80,000	1	$30,000	$25,000	10 months
Marketing Generated Mid-Size	36	$200,000	3	$75,000	$23,333	11 months
Marketing Generated Enterprise	24	$205,000	2	$75,000	$35,000	11 months

We could now analyze how much progress we were making over time against our ICPs and top segments.

CONNECTING TO BUSINESS OUTCOMES

The last thing we needed to do was connect Marketing's impact to overall business outcomes to understand how much support was actually needed.

As a reminder from the Introduction chapter of this book, David's goal for the year was to close $3M in new ARR. ClearTrack had only thirty SQLs and $750K in pipeline when he pulled up the report in Salesforce.

As we broke down the numbers further, here's what we learned about the ClearTrack business:

- The Average Deal Size for its ideal customers was $25,000
- Blended CAC Payback Period was 7 months
- Opportunities Closed at a rate of 33 percent
- Demo to Opportunity rates were 25 percent
- Net Revenue Retention was 95 percent
- LTV was hovering around 6 years

To close $3M in new ARR, ClearTrack needed at least 360 SQLs and $9M in opportunities (33 percent conversion) and 1,440

MQLs (25 percent conversion). And these numbers assumed conversion rates would hold as more volume entered the funnel.

"We need to stay on top of how we are trending in terms of pipeline coverage at all times," I said to David.

This meant constantly tracking how much volume and pipeline ClearTrack needed at all stages of the funnel versus its actual numbers. I worked with Katie to build a new dashboard for the team to report on. The key was to make sure the pipeline metrics were tying back to the overall business outcomes needed.

Given that ClearTrack needed 360 SQLs and 1,440 MQLs on the year, this meant it needed to generate at least 30 SQLs and 120 MQLs per month. This gave us a baseline to measure ongoing pipeline coverage on a monthly basis. It also gave Katie and her team exact targets to work toward.

	MQLs	SQLs	Pipeline $	Deals	Revenue
Expected	120	30	$750,000	10	$250,000
Actuals	56	14	$350,000	5	$115,500

As a reminder, ClearTrack was already generating about fifty-six demos per month, from the listed segments below.

Verticals and Segments	Avg. Demos per Month
Engineering	5
Architecture	7
Consulting	4
Legal	3
Accounting	2
Construction	3
SaaS	10
Micro (<5 seats)	22

The problem was that more than 30 percent of these demos were coming from smaller customers, which were not large enough to reach the expected requirement of $9M in pipeline for the year. Not only that, but more than 50 percent of those demos were from the wrong-fit verticals.

Based on this, I asked Katie to build a pipeline coverage model that helped us understand the breakdown by segment, including new customers, top verticals, and existing customers, along with bad-fit verticals and Micro accounts.

	MQLs	SQLs	Pipeline $	Deals	Revenue
Total Expected	120	30	$750,000	10	$250,000
Total New Customers	56	14	$350,000	5	$115,500
Total Top Verticals	16	6	$190,000	3	$85,000
Total Bad-Fit Verticals	35	5	$75,000	1	$15,000
Total Micro (<5 Seats)	22	3	$30,000	1	$15,000

With this segmentation in place, we now had a clear framework to understand how effective and focused Marketing's efforts were and how they were helping us achieve overall company objectives.

"We've finally got all the pieces in place," I said to Katie.

"To do what exactly?" she asked.

"We are finally ready to ask for more budget to help us scale faster."

9

TEAM AND BUDGET

"How much more budget do you think you'll need?" asked David, sounding concerned. "I just don't want to start burning cash."

David's concern was reasonable. A lot of software companies burn cash by overhiring and overspending on marketing efforts. David had been quite disciplined in his approach, and it was one of the reasons why ClearTrack was profitable. Because he had bootstrapped the company, cash flow and EBITDA margins were things he had always kept in mind.

In being financially disciplined, however, David had almost been too conservative in ramping up his Marketing efforts. If you recall from the Introduction, here is where ClearTrack stood as a business:

- $7M in revenue
- The Average Deal Size for its ideal customers was $25,000
- Blended CAC Payback Period was 7 months
- Opportunities Closed at a rate of 33 percent
- Demo to Opportunity rates were 25 percent
- Net Revenue Retention was 95 percent
- LTV was hovering around 6 years
- YoY growth was 15 percent
- EBITDA margins were $700K or about 10 percent
- Cash on hand was about $1.2M

With these kinds of fundamentals, it was perfectly reasonable to ramp up Marketing spend. For example, the Blended CAC Payback Period of seven months would allow ClearTrack to invest more into Marketing to drive more pipeline and recover the upfront cost of Marketing within the same rolling seven-month period as the month of investment. What David didn't realize is that he could ramp up his Marketing spend, pipeline, and revenue growth without his cash reserves going down for longer than a year.

"We've done all the heavy lifting, so this part is actually quite simple," I said to David. "This is where all the work we've done now comes together."

A lot of companies overcomplicate this phase, which slows them down and prevents them from investing in the things that make a meaningful impact on revenue.

Before exiting the business to an acquisition, founders like David need to be convinced that the value creation plan is strong enough to risk additional capital. The better the value creation plan, the more aggressively the founder can invest. In ClearTrack's case, all the work we had done to this point was to help the business build a better marketing strategy and a plan to scale the business faster and make revenue more predictable.

By being more aggressive now, David could capture significantly more enterprise value when it came time to exit.

To figure out how much more aggressive David could be, we needed to align on three things:

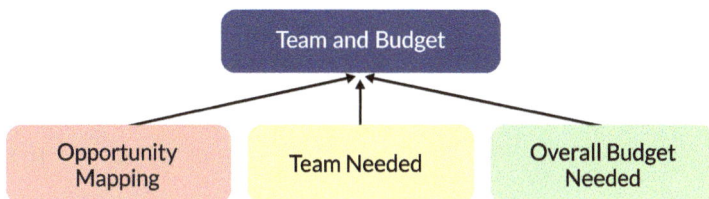

1. **Opportunity Mapping:** Of all the programs we identified, which ones should ClearTrack pursue, how much would they cost, and what would the ROI be?

2. **Team Needed:** What is the right-sized Marketing organization required to capture those opportunities?

3. **Overall Budget Needed:** How much total Marketing budget would be required across programs and headcount?

"We've identified so many opportunities already," said David, overwhelmed. "Where should we start?"

"We should focus on the initiatives that will drive the most enterprise value for the business," I said to David.

OPPORTUNITY MAPPING

As it stood, ClearTrack's Marketing program spend was about $1 million. This represented about 17 percent of revenue, which is a reasonable amount. We wanted to increase that budget to generate more pipeline and revenue, so we needed good data as an explanation.

I sat down with Katie to analyze the identified programs and channels where we wanted to invest. We created a prioritized list of opportunities, the amount of revenue associated with those opportunities, and what the return on investment would be.

"Didn't we already do all this work?" asked Katie. "It feels repetitive."

"Yes, we did some of it as part of our process," I responded. "But to lobby for more budget and convince David to invest more into this, our story has to be ironclad."

Program	Description	Additional Investment Required	Revenue Opportunity	Priority
Paid Media and SEO	Reallocate existing spend from inefficient channels to more efficient ones.	None	$65,000	High
Paid Media	Maximize existing channels, launch new programs, and channels for top verticals	$65,000	$55,000	High
SEO	Scale content for top verticals for organic search	$85,000	$70,000	Medium
ABM	Build 1-to-Few campaigns for top verticals	$1,137,000	$1,960,000	High
ABM	Build 1-to-1 campaigns for top target accounts	$991,000	$1,320,000	Medium
Customer Marketing	Expand seats from existing customers	$50,000	$1,100,000	High
Customer Marketing	Increase prices for existing customers	$15,000	$1,280,000	High
Customer Marketing	Capture payments revenue	$100,000	$1,540,000	Low

"It is crazy to see months of work all in one table," said David.

He was right. All the work we had done in the previous chapters led to this simplified, prioritized list of value creation initiatives for the business. The process takes time to get through, but as you get to the end, you see the value of all the steps in between.

"The one thing about this list that you'll notice," I said to David, "is the amount of investment required to fund all of it is just too much for where the business is today. Instead of trying to fund all of it, we will need to ruthlessly prioritize."

"I noticed that," said David. "I want to do all of it."

"We will get to all of it eventually," I explained. "First we need to scale revenue with the initiatives that produce the highest return in the shortest period of time. Then, we will get to the rest or bring the business to an investor to help us capture the rest."

In ClearTrack's case, it meant taking the above opportunities and narrowing the focus on everything listed with a High priority. We also adjusted the amount of budget allocation to the respective programs within the constraints of the current business.

Program	Description	Additional Investment Required	Revenue Opportunity	Priority
Paid Media and SEO	Reallocate existing spend from inefficient channels to more efficient ones	None	$65,000	High
Paid Media	Maximize existing channels, launch new programs, and channels for top verticals	$65,000	$55,000	High
ABM	Build 1-to-Few campaigns for top verticals	$390,000	$700,000	High
Customer Marketing	Increase seats from existing customers	$50,000	$1,100,000	High
Customer Marketing	Increase prices for existing customers	$15,000	$1,280,000	High

SCALING THE TEAM

Now that we had identified the opportunities where we were going to focus, we needed to hire someone to help Katie execute our plans. At the time, Katie only had two other marketers on her team. Both were generalists who executed on the required Marketing tasks. This meant that none of them had enough time to be more strategic or focus on an additional area.

"The overwhelm you were experiencing before was a symptom of your team not having enough people," I explained to Katie. "We're going to change that."

Katie and I worked together to figure out how many people she needed to deliver on our chosen focus areas. Katie was running a skeletal marketing organization with no actual structure. It was all hands on deck, all the time. So, we built a hiring roadmap to prioritize which roles would change that.

Role	Description	Cost	Priority
Demand Gen Marketer	• Scale Paid Media spend • Ramp up ABM programs	$120,000	High
Content Marketer	• Create content for top verticals • Create content for ABM programs	$100,000	High
Lifecycle Marketer	• Scale Customer Marketing programs • Partner with the Sales team on expansion revenue opportunities	$120,000	High
Marketing Ops Manager	• Streamline data tracking • Build automated dashboards	$100,000	Medium
SEO Content Writer	• Create organic content for top verticals and segments	$80,000	Medium

While all the identified roles were important, the first three were the most critical. On SEO and data tracking, Katie's existing team could figure out how to handle those tasks at a good enough level for us to scale. On Demand Gen, Content, ABM, and Customer Marketing, however, she needed more help.

"Getting those three people on the team would drastically improve how fast we can move through all these priorities," said Katie, excited.

"Then that's who we need to hire," I responded.

FORECASTING IMPACT

Between the three hires and the additional program spend, we had identified an additional $860K in Marketing spend for ClearTrack.

Investments	Amount	Revenue Impact
Program Spend	$520,000	$3,200,000
Headcount	$340,000	
Total	$860,000	$3,200,000

"That's almost double what we're currently investing," said David. "But I can see how much impact it's going to make on the business. We have to start getting more aggressive here."

Katie could hardly believe how easily David was willing to invest more into the business. "I never expected to get even 10 percent more, let alone almost double."

This is a common misconception Marketing leaders have of their CEOs. They think their CEOs are unwilling to spend more money or don't understand Marketing. In reality, it's the Marketing leader's job to build the right business cases to help their CEOs understand how their work will make a bigger impact on the business.

The additional $1.8M in revenue impact was also more than the $3M target David and I had initially discussed. At the time,

ClearTrack had only a fraction of the pipeline coverage it needed to hit those numbers. Now, it had a well-defined roadmap on how to get there.

David was ecstatic. "I feel like I have a much better handle on my business now."

"You're absolutely right," I said. "By doing this work, we've set up ClearTrack for success whether or not we find an investor. The more we prove this out, the more options we will have."

REVENUE GROWTH

The next 12 months at ClearTrack were a blur. Katie, Bryan, and the team relentlessly executed on all the established plans for the business. The Marketing team had grown in size, program spend had increased, and most importantly, there was more pipeline and revenue than ever before.

Zooming out, here is how the core business metrics had changed:

- Revenue jumped from $7M to $10.5M in ARR, smashing previous expectations of getting to only $10M.
- YoY growth rates were trending toward 40 percent instead of 15 percent.
- Average Deal Sizes increased to $42,000 from $25,000 as the team was doing a much better job of targeting larger accounts.
- Net Revenue Retention jumped from 95 percent to 110 percent as the Go-To-Market was focused on better-fit accounts and Customer Marketing programs expanded existing customers.
- Opportunity to Close rates increased to above 40 percent from 33 percent.
- Demo to Opportunity rates increased to 35 percent from 25 percent.
- Blended CAC Payback Period went up to 11 months from 7 months, with the increased marketing investment. But EBITDA margins increased to $1.8M or 20 percent.
- Cash on hand increased to $2.7M with the increased growth and EBITDA.

The business was thriving. ClearTrack's profile as an investment target also improved dramatically as it was now a Rule of 50 business.

Right around this time is when Pinnacle Capital reconnected with David. They wanted to check in on how things were progressing since they had last passed on the investment. When David updated them on the progress the business had made, Pinnacle couldn't throw its hat back into the ring fast enough.

This time around, there was no hesitation. The process from LOI to Close went as smoothly as possible. David also got rewarded for the work done over the last year with a significantly higher multiple due to the increased EBITDA and revenue growth rate.

"It was all worth it," said David, after the transaction closed. "I'm glad the acquisition didn't go through last year. By doing this work together, I can see now how much value we were leaving on the table."

Pinnacle Capital was also thrilled. They felt far more confident in their investment and believed they had deployed their capital in the right asset now. They continued the work David had started and kept growing the business to validate their investment thesis and return the fund.

More founders need to take their organizations through the Pyramid of Marketing Sophistication, whether or not they want to sell the business eventually. It leads to a better foundation for the entire business and makes revenue a lot more predictable.

This framework, if followed diligently, compounds over time. At How To SaaS, we take our clients through this framework every day and see phenomenal transformations over condensed periods of time.

If you are a CEO, investor, or executive who wants to take your company's marketing function through the kind of transformation we took David and ClearTrack through, schedule a consult at *www.howtosaas.com* to see how we can help your business scale faster.

RESOURCES

You can find additional resources relating to the frameworks in this book by visiting www.howtosaas.com/exit-ready-marketing-resources.

ACKNOWLEDGEMENTS

I'd like to thank the following people, who were essential in my journey to building the frameworks, experiences, and expertise shared in this book:

- Zane Tarence, Managing Director at Founders Advisors
- Michael Libert, Managing Director at TA Associates
- Bryce Youngren, Managing Partner at Polaris Growth Fund
- Donald Cowper, COO at How To SaaS
- Kate Hawkes, VP of Marketing at How To SaaS
- Gordon Cheng, Video Marketing Manager at How To SaaS
- Our entire team at How To SaaS, with whom the concepts in this book were built
- Our clients at How To SaaS, whom we get the pleasure of serving every day
- My daughter, Lyla, for inspiring me to chase my dreams

ABOUT THE AUTHOR

Shiv Narayanan is the Founder & CEO of How To SaaS, a management consulting firm that works with leading private equity investors, founders, CEOs, and revenue leaders. As an advisor, consultant, and fractional CMO, Shiv has helped B2B companies create hundreds of millions of dollars in enterprise value with marketing and demand generation. He is also the bestselling author of *Post-Acquisition Marketing* and the host of the *Private Equity Value Creation Podcast*. Previously, Shiv was the CMO of Wild Apricot, which was acquired by Rubicon Technology Partners in 2017 and flipped to Pamlico Capital in 2018.

www.ingramcontent.com/pod-product-compliance
Lightning Source LLC
Chambersburg PA
CBHW040855210326
41597CB00029B/4855